NEVER GIVE UP

A novel by

Erik Smalls

1/27/13

Chapter 1

I turned 12 on a sunny morning in 1979. Excited about my birthday, I jumped from the top of the raggedy bunk bed I shared with my brother; I couldn't wait to see the presents my parents got me. That year, my birthday fell on Labor Day, so I knew Mom would be taking me to the Labor Day Parade. Barely able to contain my enthusiasm, I ran to open the bedroom window and let the rays of sunshine into room. The morning air was crisp and refreshing—I took a deep breath.

My hair was nappy and there was still white crust itching the corners of my eyes. I was a little fat handsome boy, and most people said I looked like my mother. I was barefoot, wearing my dingy white Superman underwear and no T-shirt. I didn't like to wear T-shirts—they made me uncomfortable—even though I should've worn one to keep the bedbugs from eating me.

I walked quickly to the bathroom, badly feeling the urge to urinate. I knocked on the door but there was no answer, so I walked in only to discover my father sitting on the toilet with a needle protruding from his arm. His eyes were wide open and white—even the pupils. He had a smile on his face and a long stream of dry blood coming from the needle to his forefinger. I'd never seen anything like it before. I called to him, "Dad?" but he didn't answer. I called him again, "Daddy?"—no answer. Then I went to nudge him, but when I touched his dark skin it felt different. It didn't feel natural. His skin was cold and clammy. I began to panic and I screamed, "Daddy!" waking my brother and mother.

They both came rushing into the bathroom wearing their old dingy bedtime clothes that had clearly been washed too many times. Mom was wearing a pink nightgown with a blue belt and her hair was tied up with a blue rag. She was so pretty, even first thing in the morning. My brother was wearing his blue Superman underwear and a white tank top undershirt. He was a shade darker than me and about two inches taller.

My mother quickly shoved me aside and shook my father violently. She started screaming, a deafening sound that filled the air. Then my mother began hitting him and cursing at him.

"You can't leave me like this motherfucker! Wake up, wake up!" My mother fell to her knees as she half screamed, half sobbed, "Ricky, dial 911 quick!"

I ran to the phone in her bedroom because it was the closest and dialed 911. The dispatcher asked, "What's the emergency?"

"I think my father is dead."

"What's your address?"

"365 Fountain Avenue."

"Why do you think your father is dead?"

"There's a needle sticking out of his arm and he's not moving."

"Is there another adult in the house?"

"Yes, my mom is in the bathroom with him."

"We'll send an ambulance immediately."

After hanging up the phone I heard Mom yelling, "Peter, you don't need to see this, go to your room!"

When I came out of my parent's bedroom, my brother was just standing in front of the bathroom entrance in shock. He had a single tear rolling down his cheek and a dazed look in his eyes, as if he had lost touch with reality. I squeezed between my brother and the hallway wall to go sit down on our old worn out green sofa in the living room that should have been

4

thrown away years ago. It had holes on the armrest and a yellow cloud of dust rose up from the couch every time anyone sat on it. I just sat there thinking, lost in my own little world. I realized. *All the rumors the other kids in the projects used to tease us about are true.* When we played the Dozens, an exchange of insults between two parties, they would say, "I saw your father on Logan Avenue nodding out. Your father is a dope fiend." It was a birthday I will never forget.

Finally, about 45 minutes later, there was a knock at the door. I looked through the peephole. Two white men in blue uniforms were standing outside. Usually when white people came to our neighborhood, which was one of the worst sections of Brooklyn, they were either social workers, policemen, or EMS workers. In this case, they were with EMS. One of the men carried a black bag and the other carried a notepad. I let them in and pointed to the back without saying a word. They quickly walked to the back of the house where my father's body was. They couldn't get past my brother, who just stood motionless in the middle of the narrow hallway. I had to walk to the back to help them.

I took my brother's hand and pulled him into our bedroom. The dazed expression stayed on his face as I guided him to the bedroom. I returned to the bathroom where my mother stood sobbing and talking to the two young EMS workers.

"Do you know what was in the syringe?" I heard one of them ask.

"He's a heroin addict; I'm sure it was heroin," she replied as she wiped the tears from her face with toilet tissue. After asking her several more questions, they wrapped my father's body in a white sheet. I guessed it really made no sense to try to revive him as I had seen others revived on television so many times. My father was dead.

About an hour after the body was taken away my mom got a phone call from the coroner's office. They asked her a series of questions pertaining to funeral arrangements. Thankfully, my father had very good insurance because he worked for the city. That really helped my mom out.

I stayed in the house for the rest of the day, trying my best to console my brother and mom. My brother still hadn't said a word since my gruesome discovery. I made soup for my grief-stricken mother and a bowl of Bryer's cherry vanilla ice cream for my brother. I knew that life would be much different without my father. I thought, *Maybe this isn't such a bad thing after all.* At least I would no longer hear my mom screaming at night because my dad was beating her, a sound I dreaded and hated. The rage and anger I felt for my father in those moments was unbearable. I hated him for what he did to my mother, but it was

finally over.

Chapter 2

Dad's funeral was held at Mack's Funeral Parlor on Sutter Avenue; that's where all of the poor people in my neighborhood were prepared for burial. We pulled up to the funeral home in a long black Cadillac provided by the funeral home. I sized up my mother and brother before getting out of the car. They looked like they were going to make it through the funeral. I felt emotionally stable, but in the back of my mind, I was worrying about how we would survive on my mom's income alone.

The door opened and we exited the car. My mother, brother, and I walked slowly towards the entrance of the funeral home along with other close family members. When we reached the entrance, I held the door open for my mother and my brother entered right after her. Suddenly, my brother stopped walking.

"What's the matter?" I asked.

"I can't walk; I can't feel my legs," he replied in a low voice as if he was about to cry.

He collapsed and his nose started bleeding. My aunts and uncles ran over to help him. My uncle Ben picked him up and sat him on the couch.

I could hear my uncle ask as I walked towards the second door, "Are you OK? I know you're upset. Do you think you can go through with this?"

"I can't, I can't do this," my brother answered. "That's not my father in there, that's a corpse. I don't wanna remember him like that!" Peter cried.

Although my brother was a mess, I understood how he was feeling. He was right; that body inside wasn't my father. I approached the second door and held it open for my grieving mother, holding her hand every step of the way. My mother and I were escorted to the front row of seats. My closest family members sat directly behind us and on each side of us. I pulled a packet of tissues out of my front jacket pocket, wiped my mother's tears, kissed her cheek, and hugged her. I caressed her back in an attempt to ease her pain as the ushers were trying to seat all the mourners. When everyone was seated and the room was quiet, I looked around. There were many faces that I didn't recognize. An adult woman and three teenagers sitting all the way in the back of the room caught my gaze. They stood out because they weren't talking to anyone around them and no one was talking to them. The woman was crying uncontrollably. It was obvious that she was the mother of the three teenagers who sat with her. When the preacher began the sermon, it temporarily took my mind off the incongruous group.

The sermon went on for about 20 minutes before the woman approached my mother from behind. She introduced herself as Patricia Washington. She whispered, "Excuse me Miss, I am so sorry to hear about your loss and I know this is a bad time to tell you, but I feel you should know now." I wanted to know what could possibly be so urgent. Why did this woman have to speak to my mother right now, at the most painful moment of her life? I remember the words she said next as if it happened yesterday. She continued, "Those kids over there are a product of James."

Despite my mother's grief, she remained calm. She put her hand on her head and sighed.

"I knew he was cheating on me, but I didn't know to what extent," my mother replied as she dried her eyes. Patricia was crying just as much as my mother. My mother whispered back, "I'll talk to you after the funeral."

I could tell my mother wasn't very happy about the discovery of my father's illegitimate family, but there was nothing she could do about it. After Patricia

12

returned to her seat, I consoled my mother a little more, rubbing her back and kissing her cheek.

Finally, the preacher finished preaching. He asked if anyone had any words they wanted to share about the deceased, giving me and my mother the first opportunity. My mom declined, but I went up to the podium and spoke about the man that I had hardly known. I was as truthful as possible. I didn't shed a tear. In the middle of my speech, I put down the paper that I was reading from and spoke to the audience straight from my gut. I let everyone know of the pain that I felt due to my loss.

"My father made sure we had a roof over our heads and food on the table," I said. "He made sure I had Christmas gifts every year. He never missed a year. My father instilled principles in me that will last my whole life. Although we didn't have the typical father-son relationship, I loved him very much and I am deeply hurt."

I remember the internal turmoil I was feeling while speaking. I was being completely truthful in some ways, but at the same time I was careful not to reveal the things he did that I hated him for, as I felt those secrets should be kept within the family. I spoke to the audience about what the man lying in the coffin meant to me and my family for about ten minutes. I gave them the bitter along with the sweet. When I was done, I received a standing ovation.

Many people came up to the podium after my eulogy to share kind words about my father, but I didn't register any of their words. My mind was elsewhere. All I could think about was meeting my half brother after the funeral. I wasn't concerned about meeting my half sisters or having any more interactions with their tactless mother.

When the funeral was over, my mother and I walked out of the building hand in hand. We stood out front for about ten minutes. Mom greeted all of my father's friends, our family, and people she didn't know. My father's mistress walked out shortly after us, my half brother and sisters right behind her.

Patricia Washington was an attractive brown-skinned woman with shoulder-length black, wavy hair. She had a curvy yet slender figure. She wore a long black dress, a black bonnet, and a pair of black patent leather pumps. Her daughters, who introduced themselves as Charlene and Cheryl, were also very pretty. They wore their hair in fresh cornbraids that fell to the middle of their backs. The older of the two stood about three inches taller than her sister. They were both dressed in black linen dresses cut just below their knees, white knee high stockings, black windbreaker jackets, and patent leather shoes. My half brother was

15

dark-skinned with brown eyes and a short afro. He was the tallest of the three kids, so I assumed he was the oldest. He wore a navy blue two-piece suit that was too small for him. I could see his white socks showing when I looked at his old and worn out black leather Clarks Wallabee Shoes.

Patricia walked over to my mom and started a conversation.

"Pleased to meet you," she said with a raspy voice, as if she'd been crying all day.

"Want a cigarette?" Mom asked as she handed Patricia a pack of Marlboros.

"No thanks, I got some," Patricia answered.

I walked over to my half brother, totally ignoring Patricia and my half sisters. I introduced myself by simply saying my name, "Rick," and extending my hand.

"Devon," he replied as he grabbed my hand and gave me a firm handshake.

"So Papa was a rolling stone, huh?" I chuckled.

"Yeah, looks that way," Devon agreed.

"Where you from?"

"Seth Low Projects," he answered, as if he was proud to be from Seth Low.

"What school you go to?" I continued asking questions just to make conversation.

"Hillcrest."

"That's in Jamaica, huh?"

"Yeah, on Highland Boulevard. I'm about to go smoke a joint, man. You wanna smoke?" Devon asked as he looked around to see if anyone was close enough to hear him.

"Yeah, where you wanna go?" I responded. I didn't smoke, but it seemed like the coolest answer I could give.

"Around the corner in the park."

We walked around the corner, and as we approached the park Devon pulled out a small yellow manila envelope filled with marijuana and a package of Bamboo. My father used to send me to his supplier to pick up his weed for him. They gave it to me in the same kind of yellow envelopes that Devon had in his hand, so I used this knowledge to show Devon that I was hip.

"Where you get that from, Blake Ave?" I asked.

"Naw, my man gave it to me. He sells the shit. But I do know about that spot, Blake and Montauk."

"Yeah, the brown door," I answered. I was happy because I knew something about the streets.

We stopped and sat down on one of the park benches, and Devon skillfully rolled a joint. He lit it, passed it to me, and I took it with my forefinger and thumb the same way I had watched my father do on so many occasions. I took a puff and immediately had a coughing fit. I guess it wasn't hard to tell that I wasn't a smoker. I wouldn't really start smoking weed until a few years later. I passed the joint back to Devon, wiped the tears from my eyes, and continued coughing from the strong smoke. He laughed at me for about two minutes before taking a few more puffs as if he was a professional smoker.

We hit it off from the beginning despite my embarrassing coughing fit. We enjoyed some of the same music. He liked Gangster rap as much as I did. Ice Cube and Scarface were both of our favorite rappers. We were interested in 3the same cars and clothes to.

When we went back to the funeral home the crowd was thinning out and people were saying goodbye to my mom and brother. Devon and I exchanged phone numbers right before Patricia hugged my mother and said goodbye to my brother and me.

From that day forward I knew Devon and I were going

to be a tight-knit pair.

Chapter 3

I finally felt free from the shadow of my father's rage. I didn't have to worry about the big bad wolf any more. Things were changing for the better, or so I thought. After several weeks of living on mom's single paycheck, I began to understand why my mother had stayed married to my father for 15 long and unhappy years. My dad was a financial asset. Even though he did not make a lot of money, he was the breadwinner for the family. Each week living on a single paycheck felt harder and harder. Food was scarce before Dad's departure, but things got worse with every passing day. Our refrigerator rarely had more than five items in it. Living in poverty was normal for us. I never saw any other way of life except on television shows like *Eight is Enough* and *Happy Days*. It seemed like only white folks lived "normal lives." It seemed that they had all the necessary things to raise a child like nutritious food, nice clothes, and good schools. I'll always remember that 2 gallon glass pitcher of water that came from the tap. Mom used to have a fit if someone drank the water and didn't fill the pitcher back up.

Mom woke up at 6 a.m. faithfully every morning to go to work as a waitress at the Delwood Diner on Linden Blvd, on the border of Brooklyn and Queens. Before leaving, she would leave a dollar for Peter and a dollar for me on the old, rickety, three-legged table that we had propped up on the radiator to balance it. Sometimes it was only fifty cents or a quarter. I knew things were really bad when there was nothing at all on the table. She would put my money on one side of the table and my brother's on the other. I think she did that to avoid confusion, but we fought over the money anyway. Despite everything we were going through, my mother managed to keep a roof over our heads and some kind of food on the table. I thought, *One day I'm going to help her. Somehow, I am going to get us out of this ghetto.*

Mom always stressed the importance of a good education to me, saying, "A good education is the key to escaping the ghetto." I heard the same thing repeated by my teachers in IS 218, the intermediate school I attended just across the street from where I lived. I didn't like school. I was a very defiant child, and I balked at most of the things I was required to do for school, either because I didn't want to do them or I didn't think I was good at them. At home, getting me to take the garbage out, clean my bedroom, or do my homework was like pulling teeth. I just wasn't interested.

"Ricky, run over to Mrs. Thompson's and get me four slices of bread!" Mom yelled as she walked to her bedroom. She looked like she had a rough day at work, so I did as I was told even though I hated begging.

In the projects, some of families stuck together and others focused only on their own well-being. The Thompson family was one of the families that often pitched in to help. I knocked on the Thompsons' door with the old brass knocker that hung just above eye level in the middle of the green door. It was coming off its hinges and it had been like that for months. The maintenance crew took their time fixing things in our neighborhood. I heard a woman's voice. I knew it was Ms. Thompson, I recognized her voice.

"Who is it?" Mrs. Thompson yelled.

"Rick," I answered.

"Just a minute, baby."

There was a short pause and then I heard the sound of her slippers dragging on the floor as she slowly walked to the door, unlocked it, and opened it. The door made a terrible squeaking noise as it opened.

"Hi baby, how you doing? Mushy in the back, go on back there," Mrs. Thompson said as she opened the door wider so I could enter. She was so sweet; she treated my brother and me as if we were her own children.

I stepped in and stopped at the kitchen entrance, "No, I'm not here for Mush today, my mom sent me to see if you could spare four slices of bread."

"Sure baby, just a minute." Mrs. Thompson walked over to the sink and washed her hands before grabbing the half-empty loaf of bread that was on top of the refrigerator. She also grabbed a napkin off the table. Mrs. Thompson neatly wrapped four slices of bread in the napkin and handed them to me. "Tell your mama I said 'hey,'" Mrs. Thompson said as she opened the door to let me out. I walked back down the hall to our apartment and put the bread in the refrigerator. Mom

made my brother and me sandwiches that evening, but I

didn't see her eat anything. I very rarely saw Mom eat.

I finished my sandwich quickly because it was Saturday

evening, and on Saturday evenings one of the local DJs

set up his equipment in the park. My friends and I were

going to party in the park once again.

Normally, I would have had to ask for

permission to go to the park after the sun went down,

but the rules were a little different now that Dad wasn't

around. After finishing my dinner, I headed for the

elevator. While waiting for the elevator, I heard

screams coming from the Thompsons' apartment. I

thought, *Oh God, here we go again.* Mr. Thompson was

home and he was beating on Mrs. Thompson again. I

hated hearing their fights, but over time I had become

hardened to the sounds that came from the Thompsons'

apartment. I felt bad for Mrs. Thompson, but I had

learned very early on to control my emotions after hearing the same sounds coming from my parents' bedroom so many times. I used to just ignore them and try to fall back asleep. Sleep was always a welcome refuge from cold reality.

The sounds of couples arguing and fist-fighting were commonplace in the projects. All of my friends either came from broken homes or had parents who were abusive to them or to one another. I wondered if the adults in my neighborhood knew that the kids were watching, paying attention to them, and witnessing their rage. I wondered if they knew that their children would carry those memories for a long time, possibly for the rest of their lives. Did they know that they were shaping and molding us and they were leading by example? Did they even care?

The elevator finally arrived, and I stepped in and closed the door on the Thompsons' misery only to be greeted by the awful stench of human urine. I avoided the fluorescent yellow puddle in the middle of the floor by staying close to the graffiti-covered wall. I pushed the button for the first floor and held my breath for the thirty second journey to the lobby. I cursed under my breath as the elevator came to a stop on the third floor, which meant I'd have to breathe in the toxic fumes because I couldn't hold my breath very long. The elevator door rolled open to reveal another door, the entrance door and Cool waiting in front of the door.

Cool was at least ten years older than me. He was dark skinned, about six feet tall and approximately two hundred twenty pounds of muscle. Cool was also a real bully. Cool stepped in, avoiding the puddle. I tried to run past him, but I wasn't fast enough. He grabbed me and threw me up against the wall as the elevator door closed. I knew the drill, so I immediately took my fighting stance. Cool delivered a series of left hooks and right crosses to my body. He yelled, "Fight back!" I gave him all I had, but I was no match for him. Cool was much bigger and stronger than me and so he kicked my ass as he always did when he caught me. The elevator stopped and we stopped exchanging punches. I ran past him and down the three steps that lead to the exit of the building. When I got far enough away from him, I turned and yelled, "Fuck you, Cool!"

"You won't be saying that when I catch your ass again!" Cool yelled back.

As I walked across the grass, I heard the bass from the music coming from the DJ's powerful speakers. The DJ was playing my favorite song, "Flash Light" by Parliament. My friends always teased my brother when that song came on because he had a white spot on each of his front teeth. They said he had two lights in his mouth, so everyone pointed at him and sang the song to him when it came on. It was all in fun.

Those years were the beginning of the rap era, and many kids in my neighborhood wanted to be rappers. Some of the most popular recording artists at the time were Jam Master Flash and the Furious 5, Spoony G, Kurtis Blow, and the Sugar Hill Gang. The Bronx was the first borough to produce rappers and break-dancers. The rappers, DJs, and dancers from the Bronx were considered to be the original hip hop pioneers, but they made up only 10 percent of the musicians on the scene. They were role models to me. The other 90 percent were stickup artists. They were the people in the projects who were focused only on their own personal gains. Although I knew that positive role models existed, I didn't know much about them. I knew about Martin Luther King, Jr. and Malcom X, but those role models weren't talked about much in my neighborhood. They weren't even talked about much in school. The toughest stickup kids and best rappers were the most prominent role models for my peers.

Each borough had a different reputation. The Bronx was known for music, Brooklyn was known for stickup kids, Manhattan was known for drug dealers, Queens was known for pretty women, and no one ever spoke about Staten Island. It was as if Staten Island didn't exist.

Chapter 4

I liked hanging out with my neighbor Mush, the youngest of the Thompson kids. His real name was David Thompson. I never thought to ask him why he was nicknamed Mush. Mush had short red hair, brown eyes, and, at 5'10", stood about two inches taller than me. One day, I spotted Mush walking through the projects with an old 32-inch television precariously balanced in his arms.

"Rick, come help me, man!" Mush yelled.

I walked over to him. "Where you taking that thing?" I asked.

"To the television repair shop on Pitkin Avenue. I get five dollars for every television I bring, whether it works or not. Give me a hand and I'll split it with you."

Mush didn't have to ask me twice. I picked up one side of the television and we slowly walked to

Pitkin Avenue. We walked through the front of projects. That is what we called the side of the projects that was on Sutter Avenue, The Front. We passed the red white and blue monkey bars just before we exited the projects on Sutter. There was a gas station across Sutter on the left and a small bodega on the right. Once we got to Sutter Ave we sat the television down for a while and got a little rest. Pitkin Avenue was at least 6 long blocks up Euclid Avenue. After resting we continued up Euclid Avenue, both of us grunting, panting and sweating. We stopped to catch our breath every two or three blocks.

"Man, is this dude really gonna give us five dollars?" I asked Mush while we rested at the corner of Hegamen Street and Euclid Ave.

"Yeah, he gave me five dollars for one last Friday."

My back ached and I was developing blisters on my hand. My body was telling me to give up.

"Come on Rick, we can do it. Just four more blocks," Mush encouraged me. He picked up his side of the television again and I reluctantly picked up mine.

We carried the television two more blocks before I yelled, "Ahhh, put it down, put it down!" because the bottom of the television was cutting into my left palm. "Switch sides," I said.

Our task was further complicated because it was rush hour, and we had to dodge around the people walking from the Euclid Avenue train station on Pitkin and Euclid.

"Mush, is this dude even open? It's already five o'clock!" The last thing I wanted was to do all of that work for nothing.

"Yeah, don't worry Rick, we good," Mush assured me.

When we finally made it to Pitkin Avenue, we put the television down one last time while we waited for the traffic light to turn green.

"It's right over there," Mush pointed.

"Where?" I didn't see it.

"Over there on the corner, see the brown sign?" Mush asked, pointing again.

I spotted a little shop on the corner with a brown sign on top. The sign had small white letters on it, but I couldn't make out what it said. The lights were out and the gates were halfway down.

"Man, that shit looks closed," I said.

Mush didn't reply, so I knew that we had probably wasted our time. I wanted to drop the television right there in the middle of the street but I still retained a glimmer of hope.

We put the television down. Mush went under the gate and yelled, "Chico!" as he frantically banged on the door.

I sat on the television and inspected my blistered hands.

After about five minutes of Mush's banging I yelled, "He ain't there!"

Mush finally gave up and came out from behind the gate with a sorry look on his face.

"Man, we did this shit for nothing!" I looked at Mush. He just hung his head low and didn't answer. I was furious. Both of us were panting and drenched in sweat.

"I'm going home." I got off the television and started to cross the street. I was just as broke as I had been before I started my journey, but now, not only was I was broke, I was also exhausted and in pain.

"Hey Papi, what you got for me?"

Mush and I turned around to see a man coming from under the gate. The look on Mush's face told me that he was just as surprised as I was.

"We brought you something, Chico," Mush managed to gasp out in between breaths.

"I see," Chico said as he lifted the gate open and picked the television up with ease. Chico carried the television to the back of the shop and placed it on top of a wooden desk filled with television parts. We entered the shop after him, but stayed in the front part of the shop before the counter.

He grabbed a screwdriver that was hanging among many other tools on the wall in front of him and skillfully opened up the television. He blew inside the television casing and a huge cloud of gray dust escaped, most of it landing on his already dirty T-shirt.

While Chico was inspecting the television, Mush and I looked around at all the neat gadgets that were lying around. There were tools, wires, cables, and other things I didn't recognize, but they looked intriguing.

Chico walked over to the cash register and pushed a few buttons. I heard the drawer open. He took out a crisp five-dollar bill and handed it to Mush.

"Ya'll split that," said Chico.

I thought, *This is great, we just made five bucks!* Mush reached up and grabbed the five dollars and headed for the door.

I started thinking fast. I realized that I needed to establish my own connection to Chico, because I needed him or someone like him in my life. I needed to find a way to make him remember me or to somehow signal to him that I would be coming back to keep a long-term business relationship. I couldn't think of the right thing to say, so I just headed for the door behind

Mush. Right before I closed the door, I paused, turned, and said, "Thank you, Chico."

Chico looked at me, smiled, nodded his head and said, "You're welcome."

I knew by the look on his face that I had made the connection I needed.

Chapter 5

It was Thursday evening and my stomach was growling. The only thing in the house to eat was a half-empty box of Frosted Flakes cereal, but there wasn't any milk. I would just have to eat them with water instead. I grabbed the box out of the cupboard and filled a glass bowl half full of Frosted Flakes. As I was pouring the cereal, a cockroach scuttled for cover, trying to escape his fate. The sight of it disgusted me, but I wasn't about to let a roach stop me from eating. When the roach jumped to the floor, I stomped it, picked it up, and disposed of it in the trash can.

BOOM!! I jumped at the sound of a loud crash behind me. I turned around to see our old three-legged table lying on its side. My makeshift lunch was now a mess of broken glass, Frosted Flakes, and water covering the floor.

"GOD DAMN IT!" I yelled. Then I just stared at the mess for a few seconds before cleaning it up.

I went back to my room to play my Telstar. Telstar was one of the first video games that hooked up to the television. It was cool. All of the neighborhood kids used to come to my house to play. We had three cartridges for that game; one was Asteroids, another was Tennis, and the last was Racing Cars. I liked Tennis best because my brother and I could compete and have something to talk about later. Telstar usually helped take my mind off my situation, but it didn't help this time. My stomach was still growling.

After about two hours of playing Telstar, I heard the jingle of my mom's keys in the door. I was always glad to see her. As usual, she looked like she had a rough day.

"Hi, Ma," I looked up at her and smiled.

"Hey babe, where's your brother?"

"He's at Mush's house playing records." We used to pretend we were DJs and rappers with two turntables, a mixer, and a microphone. One of us would stand in front of the turntables and mixer with headphones on, waiting for the perfect moment to bring another beat into a track, while the other would rap to the beat. Who knows where Mush got that equipment from; it had clearly seen better days.

"Why are you not over there?"

"I was hungry."

"What did you eat? There ain't nothing in there."

"Cereal and water." I hung my head low, feeling guilty for lying. I didn't want to put more stress on her by telling her what happened to my meal. "What are we having for dinner, Ma?" I asked in an attempt to take the focus off my lunch.

"Give me a minute and I'll scrape up some change to get us some chicken wings for dinner tonight."

Mom went to the bathroom and changed into her beige shorts and white T-shirt that she always wore that around the house. I waited for her patiently in her bedroom and watched the old black-and-white television with the clothes hanger on top. The clothes hanger was a substitute for the broken antenna. When the television scrambled, we would walk up to it and smack it real hard. Sometimes a smack unscrambled it.

Mom searched what seemed like every pocket in her closet, the bottom of her purse, and in her dresser drawer for change. When she could not find any more change, she threw all of what she had gathered on her bed, sat next to it, and carefully counted it out. Mom handed me three dollars worth of change, mostly pennies.

"Run down to Julio's and get three dollars worth of chicken wings," Mom said. "And make sure you go to Julio's, 'cause he cheaper than Logan."

Normally, I would go to Logan Avenue's corner store because it was closer. I put all the change mom gave me in one back pocket and headed for the door. I ran down five flights of stairs using the new trick of skipping steps that I learned from Mush. Julio's was on Sutter Avenue, just two and a half blocks from my house.

"Rick!" Someone called me from across Fountain Avenue. It was my neighbor, José. José lived in the building facing mine. He played with us when he was around, but he was rarely around. He was one of the first of the kids in my peer group that had gone to prison, and it seemed like he made prison his second home because he spent more time there than in the neighborhood.

I knew José was up to no good, he always was. Some said he was not quite right in the head. José was a big Puerto Rican. He wore his hair in thick braids and stood about six feet tall. He had a tear drop tattoo on his face and a gold tooth in his mouth. At that time, having a gold tooth was one of the latest fad s that the stick up artists brought to our neighborhood. I eventually got one. I reluctantly walked over to José. I knew it would only mean trouble if I said no, as he would just come to me instead.

The last time José was home from prison, he strong-arm robbed my cousin for his movie money. I never understood why the stick up kids in the projects robbed their neighbors. Why did we rob each other when all of us were poor?

"Empty your pockets, Rick!" José demanded in his Spanish accent.

"No, I ain't got nothing!" I began to walk away.

José grabbed me in a headlock, a choke hold I used to see on the World Wide Wrestling Federation every Thursday night. He squeezed until I was lightheaded, cutting off my oxygen and blood circulation. My knees became weak. Tears came to my eyes at the thought of not being able to eat again. My family would have to go to bed hungry again because of this asshole. He patted my pockets with his free hand and heard the sound of change, so he knew he'd hit the jackpot. Before he could put his hand in my pocket and claim his reward for all of his hard work, a strange adrenaline rush surged through my body. I managed to gather enough strength to position my mouth behind his forearm. I bit him as hard as I could.

"AAAAAHHHHH!" José let out a loud scream and let me go.

As soon as I was free, I took off running down the street. I ran two blocks past Julio's, constantly looking behind me to make sure he wasn't coming. Still very scared and dizzy, I stopped and sat on a stoop at the corner of Sutter Avenue and Milford to catch my breath. I wondered, *What will José do to me when he sees me again?* It was inevitable for him to see me again.

I got my wings at Julio's and took a different route home. Despite my dread of José's revenge, I walked back home from Julio's feeling happy. I felt like I had saved the day. We were going to have dinner that night.

Chapter 6

Prospect Park is the biggest park in Brooklyn, New York. There was a carousel in the park that I rode as an adult in a romantic moment with my partner. There was a zoo in the park that the city had to close in 1988 when a kid climbed into the polar bears' cage and was eaten by the bears. When the police arrived, they couldn't get into the cage so they watched as the kid was eaten alive. The kid's screams were heard throughout the neighborhood. When the zookeeper finally arrived to unlock the cage, the kid's entire torso had been eaten and the bears' faces were covered in blood as they fought over the remains. The cops shot the bears thirty times, six times with a service revolver and twenty-four times with shotguns. The bears' screams were heard throughout the neighborhood.

We had many family events in Prospect Park. I loved our family picnics in Prospect Park. There was a huge lake right next to our favorite picnic spot. Many of my aunts and uncles came to the picnics and they always brought plenty of food to share with the family. Devon and my half-sisters Charlene and Cheryl got along great with the extended family; everyone accepted them into the family. We played volleyball, listened to music, rode our road bikes, climbed mountains, and feasted on the delicious soul food. Devon and I also hustled water and soda to make some money.

My older cousin Clarence was always at the picnics. I thought Clarence was so cool. He had a signature style, and wore his Apple Jack cap tipped to the side, dark shades, neatly pressed jeans, and a collared shirt most of the time. Clarence was black as night and a very handsome man. All of the kids in my family looked up to Clarence. He was a real good guy. Clarence mumbled when he spoke and we usually didn't know what he was saying, but we knew whatever it was, it was cool, so we'd just nod our heads in agreement. Clarence's mother, my Aunt Ebeniza, was never far away from Clarence. Aunt Ebeniza was a pretty, chocolate-complexioned woman. She had beautiful brown eyes and curly black hair. She looked just like my Nana, but two shades darker. She was just as cool as her son.

"Ma, can I borrow 40 dollars just 'till we get back from the park?" I asked for the money so I could buy my water and beer to hustle with Devon.

"I have to stop at the bank on our way to see if my paycheck cleared." She knew what I had in mind, so she never put up a fight. Mom supported my hustle because she knew that she wouldn't have to give me money for a few days.

Devon and I walked up and down long hills of Prospect Park pulling our cooler filled with water and beer. We strapped the coolers to small hand trucks designed to carry luggage so we could roll them. The sun was shining and the parks trees and flowers were in full bloom. We shared the road with bicyclists, joggers, and other pedestrians. There was also the occasional car passing by. There were a lot of people in the park on a beautiful summer day. Everyone in the park was a potential customer for Devon and I. Who wouldn't want a cold beverage on a hot summer day?

"Ice beer, ice cold water!" Devon and I yelled loud enough of every one in hearing distance to hear us. Devon walked on the right side of the road and I walked on the left.

"How much for 2 Heinekens?" a young blonde-haired biker pulled over to ask me.

"$2.00," I replied.

The man reached in a pouch that hung from the handlebars of his gold ten speed bike and handed me $2.00. As I put the money on top of large stack of bills I saw Devon walk over to a picnicking couple to make a deal. The exchange of money for goods was great but I liked the excitement of finding the customers and making the deal more. I loved the hustle, and I was good at it.

To be able to put together a plan, execute it, and then reap the benefits was awesome. I felt there wasn't much I couldn't accomplish if I put my mind to it, as long as I could put together a plan. My beverage business was tangible proof of that.

Devon was just as good a hustler as me, and I could see Devon was enjoying himself just as much as I was. He yelled across the road to me while grabbing his pocket to show me the outline of the money he had.

"My pockets look like they got the mumps!" he laughed. Then he yelled, "Ice cold water, ice cold beer!"

It only took a few hours before we were back at the picnic enjoying ourselves and feeling good because our pockets were filled with money.

Chapter 7

My grandparents were a sweet old couple. We moved to the Crown Heights section of Brooklyn to live with them when our rent became too much for my mother to handle with one income. I was very upset when we left the projects. Moving on was hard. Every day after school I hung out with my friends before getting on the A train to go back to my grandparents' house. I didn't want to go. I didn't want to leave my friends. Even though some of my friends weren't exactly pillars of the community, they were my friends. I also liked the street credibility and status I got from living in the Cypress Hills Projects. I was a part of something, a huge team that was well-known, respected, and recognized as the toughest project in Brooklyn. Since ghetto life was all I knew I thought it was a normal way of life, and that is where I wanted to stay.

Nana stayed in the kitchen baking cookies, sweet potato pie, pound cake, and anything else that would make a kid happy. Nana had tan skin and pretty red shoulder-length hair. She stood about five feet five inches tall and was a bit on the heavy side. Everyone loved Nana, and Nana loved everyone. My grandfather was a hard-working man. He worked for Wonder Bread until he retired. He was short, brown-skinned, and always kept his hair in a neat crew cut. He wore blue jeans and a blue sweatshirt to work every day. On the weekends, he went to church in his two-piece brown suit.

I was still attending I.S. 218 in East New York while living in Crown Heights, Brooklyn. It was my last year at 218 and Mom didn't want to take me out of the school in the middle of the school year. My grandfather drove me to school in his light blue Buick Electra, known on the streets as "the Deuce and a Quarter." I really enjoyed riding to school with my hip grandfather in his cool car. For an older man, he seemed to know a lot about what went on in the streets.

"Them boys up to no good. See how they runnin'? And that one there got a gun, look how he holdin' his waist," Granddad said as we saw three young teenagers running up Blake Avenue.

It seemed as though Granddad was right. When we got to the stop sign, there was a man sitting on the curb bleeding from his head. I wondered if he had been shot. Granddad just shook his head and kept driving.

I didn't understand why Granddad wasn't pulling over to help. "Ain't we gonna help him, Granddad?"

"You see that kind of stuff, you best to just mind your business," Granddad explained.

It wasn't until years later that I fully understood what Granddad had told me. Even being from the hood, there were still a lot of things I didn't know or understand about the ghetto. We stayed at my grandparents' house for nearly two years.

****

I got a job working at Allied Maintenance when I was 17. I was so happy. It was my first job and the feeling of independence was great. I finally felt like a grown-up. Now that I was earning money, I could help Mom with our expenses.

Allied was a janitorial company that served the five boroughs of New York City. I was paid $9.66 per hour, which was considered good money back then. I worked at Two Penn Plaza in midtown Manhattan from 6 p.m. to 12 a.m. five days a week. It was a dirty job; I emptied the trash, dusted furniture, and swept and mopped floors, among other things. I really enjoyed my job even though it was a dirty job.

I managed to save enough money for a down payment on my first car. I bought it from a little car lot on Northern Boulevard in Elmhurst, Queens. It was a pretty black Nissan Maxima with a beige interior. It came with a spoiler kit and custom BBS rims. My godmother co-signed for it, and I made payments on it every month. Things were finally looking up for us.

I worked at Two Penn Plaza for six months before transferring to the Grace Building on 42nd Street and 6th Avenue in Manhattan. I was given bathroom duty at the Grace Building. The bathrooms were filthy. I couldn't believe the way people kept the bathrooms. Some had tissue and debris all over the floor because the trash cans were over-filled. I will always remember my first day at the Grace Building. I was cleaning the women's bathroom and noticed a weird box on the wall next to the toilet that looked out of place. There was a little latch on the box, so I slid the latch to the right and the box popped open. What looked like used tissues and rags fell out and onto the floor. A terrible odor wafted from the spilled refuse. I jumped back in shock and stared at the mess: used sanitary napkins were all over the floor! I had never seen or smelled anything so disgusting before. After I regained my composure, I used my broom and dustpan to clean up the mess. That same night I encountered an even worse surprise. Someone had missed the toilet and shat all over the side of the stool. I thought, *No way, this can't be happening. How the hell do you miss the fuckin' toilet? Some idiot must have done it on purpose.* I was furious. I went downstairs to the basement and told my supervisor, Mr. Mason. Mr. Mason was an older man, perhaps in his mid-fifties. He was light-skinned and had a nasty scar on his left cheek. He stood about 5'7" and wore his hair in a short Caesar cut.

"Mr. Mason, what are we gonna do? Someone shit on the floor!" I looked upset and confused.

"You have to clean it, it's your job," Mr. Mason replied.

Somehow I knew he was going say that, but I was hoping for a different answer.

"Really?" I replied, still looking confused.

"That's what we are paid to do; clean." Mr. Mason made it sound so simple.

As I rode the elevator back up to the tenth floor, I thought of ways to handle the bathroom without dealing with the shit. The tampons and sanitary napkins were one thing, but there was no way I was going to clean up human shit. I stood at the entrance of the bathroom for at least twenty minutes, thinking of something my mom used to say to me. *If you don't finish school, you'll be cleaning shit for the rest to for your life.* How ironic.

I knew that my job depended on the decision I had to make, and I knew that I didn't have much time to make it. My family needed me I had to do what I had to do. I swallowed my pride, put on my cleaning gloves, and picked up the scrub brush and spray bottle of ammonia that I had dangling from the front of my cleaning supply cart. I slowly walked back to the stall, opened the door, and stared at it again in disbelief. The shit was all dried up around the side of the stool, and there was a small pile where the stool met the floor. I turned around, walked back out, and closed the stall door. I couldn't do it. I grabbed all of my tools and cleaning supplies and went back downstairs to break the news to Mr. Mason.

"Mr. Mason," I began. "I'm sorry to waste your time, but I don't think this job is for me. I can't do this job."

"That's okay, Rick. I knew the job wasn't for you when you walked in here. Just put your equipment over there on the table, sign out, and call the office in the morning to let them know you won't be coming back," Mr. Mason replied. "You take care, Rick." He held out his hand to shake mine before I left. I shook his hand and went to the locker room to change clothes before leaving.

As I waited for the elevator I thought, *Now what am I gonna do? How will I help Mom, and how will I pay my car note?*

Chapter 8

The extra money I gave to Mom before quitting my job combined with the earnings from Mom's new job allowed her to save up enough money to get us out of my grandparent's house. We moved to Jamaica Queens. Mom rented a small one-bedroom apartment just off Parsons Boulevard, about two blocks from Jamaica Avenue Shopping Center. Coincidentally, my half-brother Devon frequented Jamaica Avenue. That's where he hustled wholesale goods after school. He sold cassette tapes, tube socks, T-shirts, and whatever else he could find to make a quick buck. Devon taught me the ropes and I began doing business on Jamaica Avenue, too.

We bought most of our merchandise from midtown Manhattan. Broadway between 25th Street and 32nd Street had the best deals. On a bad day, I would start with roughly fifty dollars and pick up fifteen T-shirts. I would go to Jamaica Ave, sell my shirts early, and be back at the wholesale spot before they closed to buy more product for the evening shift. On most days, I made between fifty and a hundred dollars in profit.

I ran into Mel on Parsons Boulevard one day after selling T-shirts all day. Mel was a light-skinned, tall, slim, young hustler. He always dressed sharp and wore the best clothes. He had light freckles in his face and he kept his hair in a Jersey-style fade with natural curls on top. He was slightly bow-legged. Mel and I became very close friends. I was fascinated by the way he could convince just about anyone to do just about anything.

I had a couple more shirts left and Mel acted as if he was a buyer, looking at the shirts, checking the size and asking the price. After about five minutes, he told me he wasn't buying, but he did know a few people that would be interested. I felt a good aura surrounding

Mel, so we walked up 89th Avenue together.

"WHOPPEN SPLIFF!" Mel yelled to a tall,

light-skinned Rastafarian with long well-maintained

dreads who was standing on 163rd Street and 89th

Avenue.

"AWHOO!" replied Spliff, acknowledging

Mel's greeting.

"Come and lick off a bumbaclot T-shirt from

me, lion!" Mel yelled back, holding a few shirts high in

the air.

"Naw Mel, cash reeeeally tight today. Dumb

beast boys knock off me gate. Cash reeeeally tight!"

"RESPECT ME LION!" Mel replied before

moving on to the next potential customer.

"He owns the Fish Market weed spot on Hillside

Ave." Mel hipped me to most of the things that went on

in the neighborhood. I later learned that since the Fish

Market weed spot was right above the fish market, it adopted the name the Fish Market.

We walked into a grocery store on the corner. There was a short, balding, Spanish man standing behind the counter. Mel threw all the shirts up on the counter.

"Check 'em out, Papi," Mel said, then walked toward the beer section of the store.

"No Puncho, no today, no have money," Papi replied.

"Papi, why you insulting me? Did I ask you for any money? All I ask you to do is check them out. C'mon, you know my brother, you deal with him all the time." Mel used his brother's name to gain Papi's confidence. I found out later that Mel's brother was a heavy drug dealer in the neighborhood.

"I'm trying to give you something for free, Papi. Check 'em out, tell me which one you want." Just as I was about to snatch my shirts, Mel turned to me and winked.

A pretty, light-skinned woman came out of the back and took notice of the shirts.

"You'll look nice in this one, Mamacita." Mel handed the woman a pink T-shirt with Minnie Mouse on the front. She smiled and appeared interested, at which point Papi began to take interest. He touched the black one that was in my hand. Mel quickly snatched the black one from me.

"Papi, try it on over your tank top," Mel insisted.

Mel turned to the woman and asked, "Mamacita, don't he look good?" She nodded her head in agreement and said something in Spanish while she inspected the pink T-shirt in her hand.

"I get ten bucks a piece for the shirts, but I'll give you five for forty dollars," Mel said.

She inspected the other shirts for about five minutes before she chose six from the pile and walked to the register and gave Mel forty dollars.

I was satisfied, but Mel just kept on bargaining.

"Come on, Mamacita. I get ten dollars a shirt, I can't take any less."

"Take it or leave it," said Mamacita.

Mel had a disappointed look on his face. "Can we at least have two beers and call it a deal?"

"Take them," Mamacita answered.

Mel picked up two Heinekens, popped the tops off, and handed one to me. When we got outside, he handed me thirty dollars. I was impressed. I have never met another salesman as good as Mel.

**** .

I walked into the Fish Market and up one flight of old noisy steps while I held on to a broken banister.

The hallway lights were dim and the aroma of high-grade weed was coming from the only apartment at the top of the steps. When I reached the top of the steps, I knocked on a gray metal door. It had dents all over it, a peephole, and another hole about the size of a quarter just above the lock cylinder. I pushed five dollars through the little hole and the door opened up. It wasn't supposed to open. My weed was supposed to be pushed back through the hole from the other side. A tall, light-skinned Rastafarian with long, well-maintained dreads was standing on the other side. He wore several gold necklaces with medallions dangling at the bottoms and his clothes were neatly pressed. I recognized him as Spliff.

"Ya want work?" Spliff asked.

"Sure," I replied.

He gestured for me to come in. As I entered, I took in my surroundings. The apartment was filthy.

There was an odor of mildew in the apartment, the paint on the walls was chipped, and there were huge holes in the walls. Two other Rastas were seated around a wooden table in the kitchen, breaking up large buds of weed to stuff into yellow manila envelopes. They were preparing the weed for sale. Someone knocked on the door.

"Come a now." Spliff wanted me to come with him.

We went to the door. "WHOPPEN STY!" Spliff yelled and took a five dollar bill from the hole.

"REGULAR!" The person on the other side of the door yelled back.

There were two large plastic baggies that hung on the wall next to the entrance. One was filled with one inch by two inch manila envelopes stuffed with regular weed. The other was filled with half inch by one inch manila envelopes stuffed with sensimilla weed.

70

Spliff put his hand in the one that contained the regular weed, took one package out, and pushed it through hole. Then we heard the customer walking down the steps.

"Ya afa keep most da money inna stash, see?" He showed me a stash over the door in between the wood that made up the entrance frame.

"Yeah," I replied.

"Hallways double lock da door, ya understand?"

"Yeah," I answered.

There were two locks on the door. One was a deadbolt and the other was a police lock. I hadn't seen a police lock since I was about five years old and living on Menahan Street in the Bushwick section of Brooklyn. The police lock was made of a five foot long metal pole. The top of the metal pole was placed under a metal two by four that was welded to the door about four feet from the bottom. The bottom of the pole was placed in front of another metal two by four that was

bolted to the floor about three feet away from the door.

The pole was wedged in between the floor and the door,

making it next to impossible to open the door from the

outside when locked.

Spliff explained a little more about the simple

job to me before making sure both bags contained

sufficient amounts of weed. He counted one thousand

dollars worth of weed in front of me, five hundred

dollars' worth of sensimilla and five hundred dollars

worth of regular. He handed me a twenty dollar bud of

sensimilla for my personal use and told me that my pay

would be two hundred dollars per day and I would be

paid daily. Then Spliff and the two other Rastafarians

packed up their things and left.

I only planned to work there for a week. It was

an opportunity to save enough money to buy two

weeks' worth of shirts without running back and forth

to midtown. I smoked weed all day and sometimes I sold some of my personal weed for a few extra dollars.

****

BOOM! Someone yelled, "OPEN THE FUCKING DOOR, IT'S THE POLICE!"

My heart felt like it was about to jump out of my chest. Every hair on my body stood on end. I moved with lightening fast speed toward the two baggies that contained the weed, grabbed them, and frantically ran to the bathroom.

BOOM, BOOM! The apartment shook twice from two more loud explosions.

"OPEN THE FUCKING DOOR!" someone in the hallway yelled again, just as I reached the toilet. I started emptying the contents of the plastic baggies into the toilet. I pushed the lever on the toilet, but it wouldn't flush. I wiggled the lever and tried again. It dawned on me that the police had shut the water off. I frantically grabbed the weed packages from the toilet and stuffed them back into the plastic baggies.

BOOM, BOOM, BOOM!! The police were still trying to get in and I was running out of time. I ran to the bedroom window.

"C'mon jump, I'll catch ya!" one of the cops yelled when he saw me look out of the window. Jumping was a bad idea. I looked around the room and noticed a hole in the wall of a closet, so I stuffed both baggies behind the sheet rock.

I walked back to the front of the apartment out of breath.

BOOM, BOOM!

"What the fuck is holding it?!" someone yelled.

The deadbolt looked like it was weakening, but the police lock stood firm.

"WAIT A MINUTE!" I yelled, and unlocked both locks. As soon as I unlocked the door, three cops rushed in.

"Get up against the wall and spread your legs," one cop ordered as the two others ran past me. All of them had their guns drawn.

"Hands behind your back!" the officer that searched me ordered.

"Where's the weed?" the cop that was searching the kitchen yelled.

The cop that cuffed me said, "Search the bathroom. His hands are wet."

I was escorted to the back of the apartment while my arresting officer asked me a series of questions. "I don't have any weed," I insisted, still out of breath.

They continued searching the apartment and trying to convince me to tell them where the weed was while I stood handcuffed in the middle of the empty bedroom. I wouldn't look at my hiding spot because I didn't want their attention directed there.

"JACKPOT!" One officer yelled. "There's a puddle growing on the floor of that closet. I'll bet my badge it's in the wall."

Chapter 9

I started seeing less of Devon. He began hanging out in Manhattan because he said there was more money there. He said some of the richest people in the United States lived in Manhattan. He stopped returning my phone calls, and months went by. Then, one weekend, I got a phone call.

"Come down stairs, we goin' out."

"Dee?" I answered.

"Yeah, come on down."

I put on my jacket and ran downstairs. I was so happy to hear from him that I smiled all the way to the first floor. By the time I got to the exit I stopped smiling. I didn't want him to know how much I missed him. It just wasn't a macho thing to do.

When I got downstairs Devon was sitting in the driver's seat of a pretty white one year old Cadillac. I didn't know what he was doing but I knew I wanted in. He had a pretty young black girl in the car. She wore a long wig, a tight-fitting brown dress, and brown open-toed high heeled shoes. Devon didn't introduce me to her but he called her Pleasure so I assumed that was her name. He drove me to 11th Avenue and 43rd Street in Manhattan, showing me around as if we were on a tour. Then he introduced me to his friends. All of his friends had nice cars, a lot of money, and pretty women to. They all called him Cashmere so from that day on I called him Cashmere too, Cash for short.

Cashmere told me he was pimping the young girl that rode with him. As we drove around the neighborhood he taught me things the average person didn't know about the streets. Some of the things he taught me I already knew from reading Donald Goings' *Whoreson* and Robert Becks' *Pimp: The Story of My Life*. He told me that I could make a lot of money if I followed his instructions. I was always interested in making money. From the outside looking in the game looked sweet. I wanted the huge bank roll, nice clothes, cars, and jewelry that I saw my older brother with.

For weeks I thought about what Cash taught and showed me, and then, once again, I made a very bad decision. If I had known then what I would go through I would have chosen a different profession. But it seemed like every time I was faced with an important decision I chose the wrong way. I dropped out of high school—wrong way. I quit my job—wrong way. I was influenced by Cashmere—wrong way. I should have been nick named Wrong Way Rick. I did the math: $300 to $400 per night peddling flesh was a hell of a lot better than $50 to $100 per day peddling t-shirts. It didn't take a rocket scientist to figure that one out.

I fantasized about what I would do with all that money. *I could by my mom a house. I would at least be able to save up for a down payment. I could probably move out and Mom wouldn't have to worry about taking care of me; she would just have to worry about Pete. To hell with a Maxima; this is Benz money!* The exposure to the lifestyle was bait for me, and I was hooked. I was all in.

I drove all over New York City looking for a woman to help me start my pimping career. My only strategy was to look for a woman that needed me. I thought of a way that I could help a woman, and I used it to my benefit. I rented a small studio apartment on Hancock Street and Franklin Avenue in the Bedford Stuyvesant section of Brooklyn with the money I made on Jamaica Avenue. I rented that place only because it was the cheapest place I could find. I had a car, I had an income, and I had shelter—the basic tools that everyone needed to survive. I just had to find a woman who didn't have those tools.

****

One Thursday night, while parked in front of the women's' homeless shelter on Mathews Street and Sutter Avenue, I saw a pretty, light-skinned girl walk out of the shelter.

"Those are some pretty green bedroom eyes you got there," I flirted from the window of my car as she passed by.

"Thank you," she replied, blushing.

"Where you goin'?" I asked. I got out of the car to show off the new Louis Vuitton outfit I bought for the sole purpose of impressing women. She noticed the outfit as soon as I got out of the car.

"Oooh, I love Louis Vuitton," she said as she touched my jacket without my permission.
"I used to buy my girlfriend Louie all the time. She loved it too," I replied, looking down sadly.

"What's the matter?"

"She left me for a hustler. Now she lives in a big house in Long Island and he spoils her rotten."

"Awww, don't be sad. She'll come back."

"I don't want her back. I just don't like the idea of living on my own now. I don't know how to cook or clean, and I get lonely."

"You live alone?" she asked, looking at me as if she'd just hit the jack pot.

"Yeah, been by myself for about three months now."

"You seem like a nice guy. Why haven't you found another girlfriend?"

"Where were you off to?" I asked, changing the subject.

"The food line down the block. They got peanut butter and jelly sandwiches today."

I have always had a passion for business. Making my own hours, being in control of my destiny, and being the boss are all things that I always dreamed of. Pimping was a business, and a very profitable one. It ran the same as any legitimate business. I'd find out where my best leads were; usually different tracks. There were at least 20 of them in New York City that I learned about from others in the business. The tracks were my leads. Although any woman was a prospect, I only pursued a select few because some needed more work than others to be marketable. Once I found the right prospect I would interview her to see if she was a good fit for my paperless contract. On the interview I'd listen to my prospect's needs and present an avenue to help her meet her goals for a consideration: money. The key to finding the right business partner was listening. Each one of the prospects was unique. Some needed shelter; some needed sex; some needed love, inspiration, and appreciation. The only way to find out what they needed was to listen carefully. I used to call it finding the keys to Pandora's Box.

Linda was hungry and probably hadn't had a decent meal in months. So she gave me at least one key: food was a starting point.

"You wanna grab a bite to eat?" I asked, gesturing with a head movement for her to get in the car.

"Sure. I'm hungry," she answered, walking toward the passenger's side.

"What's your name?"

"Linda."

"So what do you wanna eat, Linda?"

"I don't care, I'm not picky."

I took her to the Malary Diner on Linden Blvd.

We entered the diner and were escorted to our seats. After about five minutes of small talk and reading the menu a waitress approached us with a pen and pad in her hand.

"Can I take your orders?" she asked while looking at me.

"Ladies first," I insisted.

Linda ordered a pastrami and Swiss on rye with mustard. I ordered a Kaiser roll toasted with butter a small coffee.

"How do you like your coffee, sir?" the waitress asked me.

"Light and sweet, the way I like my women," I answered while looking at Linda.

Linda smiled like I knew she would. The waitress took our menus and left.

Alone with Linda, I noticed that she had a nasty burn on her shoulder. I asked her how she got it.

"My mom was abusive. I got this one for knocking over a glass of Kool-Aid when I was 10. She burned me with a hot iron. Whenever my mom was drunk, which was just about every night, she'd find a reason to whip my ass or torture me in some way. When she wasn't drunk she'd be sleepin' it off or telling me how much she loved me. I believed her, too. I was a child and that's all I knew, so I thought it was normal. I loved her with all my heart despite the abuse."

"I'm assuming that has something to do with why you ended up in the shelter?"

Linda bit her bottom lip, and then paused with her head down. When she picked her head up there was a blank expression on her face as if she was replaying an abusive scene in her head. She slowly shook her head and continued, "Mama took me to my babysitter's one morning, kissed me on the forehead, and said she'd be back in a few hours. I sat in my babysitter's house 'til midnight. The babysitter began to look worried. She started making phone calls. I wasn't worried; I knew my mama was coming back. She loved me. Finally the doorbell rang. I waited up stairs for Mama to come get me like she always did. After about five minutes Mama didn't come up so I went downstairs. When I walked into the kitchen to greet my mom there was only the babysitter and two uniformed policemen sitting at the table talking. The police took me to a group home. Mama never came and got me." Linda paused. Her whole body began to tremble, her jaw tightened, and there was a look of rage in her piercing hazel eyes. She went on, "I stayed in the group home 'til the city found a family to adopt me. I moved around in foster homes and group homes for 10 years. My foster parents raped me and whipped me in every home I went to. When I turned 18 I was allowed to live in the women's shelter. The shelter is like paradise compared to where I've been. I've been there for nearly a year. At least no one hurts me anymore." Linda stared straight ahead as if she was looking through me—a cold, callous, empty stare.

"I'm sorry, Linda." I didn't know what else to say. And I thought I had it rough.

"Don't be. That's life," Linda replied stoically.

I sat silently for a moment, wondering if I should continue my mission. There was a war going on in my soul, as if I had two consciences, one good and the other bad. The good, which I used to call my good conscience, said, *Don't continue, don't bring this poor girl more misery. Let her go*. My bad conscience, the devil in me, said, *You almost got her! Just continue, and before the week is out she will be your first catch.*

The money and material things I had been exposed to on the track got the best of me; the devil got the best of me. After hearing what happened to Linda I knew that she probably had a sexual dysfunction and didn't like men. I planned on using that information in the future. It was another key.

Our food arrived, and we ate and talked for about an hour.

"You wanna take a ride back to my house and hang out with me?" I asked.

"Sure, as long as you have me back by curfew."

"Cool," I said as I pulled the money out of my pocket to pay the bill. I made sure she saw the three $20 bills I had neatly placed on top of two hundred singles. As I did, Linda looked at the check and put it back on the table. I was glad she looked because I wanted her to know how much of a tip I was leaving.

"Eight dollars? You're leavin' too much. You should only leave ten percent of the cost of the meal," Linda said, as if I was breaking a rule.

"It's OK, they make their living off tips," I replied.

Linda looked at me as if I'd committed a cardinal sin.

"I could use some of that for breakfast," Linda exclaimed.

Before she picked it up and put it in her pocket I stood up and put my jacket on. I hoped she would do the same and she did.

As we approached the exit she looked back at the tip one last time before walking out.

I flirted with Linda on the way back to my house. I made her blush and kept her in a good mood, which wasn't hard to do. Despite her tough life, she seemed to be a very happy woman. We were getting along great.

I was a little embarrassed when we got to my house because I hadn't cleaned up, but I used it to my advantage.

"See, I told you I don't know how to clean. And I don't remember the last time I had a home-cooked meal," I said with my head down as if I was sad.

"I can clean this place for you. I could even cook you a nice meal if you buy the ingredients," she replied.

"What am I going to do when you leave?" I asked.

"I can stay here with you if you want."

There was a short silence.

"Well, OK, but there's something I have to tell you 'bout me," I said as I looked at her.

"What?"

"I don't like sex," I said, because I assumed Linda had a sexual dysfunction considering what she'd been through. There's no way such a pretty woman would have been living in a shelter for a year. I'm sure she had men pursuing her every day, and I was sure some lonely man would take her home if only for sex, if nothing else. I wanted her to feel comfortable talking about herself, and I figured that if she knew that I wasn't after her body and wasn't going to hurt her I'd get more information. .

"That's OK; I don't either. Well, not with boys anyway," Linda replied.

"Ohh, you're a seafood lover?" I asked jokingly.

"Yeah," she answered with a giggle.

We listened to music until the sun went down, then lay in bed watching the old 22 inch television my mom bought me for Christmas.

****

"Wanna go for a ride?" I asked Linda a few hours later, as I got up and put my pants on.

"Sure," she replied, getting up to get dressed.

We took a ride over to the track, 43rd Street and 11th Ave. When we got there Linda couldn't believe her eyes.

"Those girls are prostitutes!" she exclaimed in shock.

"Yeah, those girls are out here every night making money. They make anywhere from five hundred to a thousand dollars a night."

I pulled over and parked in the middle of the block so Linda could get a good look at the expensive cars the pimps had, the jewelry they wore, and the money she could be making. I got out of the car quickly so she wouldn't follow me. "Be right back," I shouted without looking at her as I slammed the door.

I walked over to Cash and spoke to him for about 15 minutes about nothing of importance, then went back to the car.

"Some girl with her ass out just hoped in a car right in front of me!" Her voice was at least 2 octaves higher than usual. Her eyes were wider than normal. Her breathing was a bit heavier, there were wrinkles on her forehead between her eyebrows, and her mouth was agape as she stared in disbelief.

"Yeah, I told you they get paid out here. That was probably my brother's girl. He was just telling me he been out here for just two hours and already checked $500," I lied.

As I pulled off down 43rd Street I glanced at Linda. She was in deep thought.

"Do you think I could do that?" Linda asked.

"Do what?" I replied, pretending I had no idea what she was referring to.

"What those girls were doin' back there."

"Hell yeah. I know you'd make way more than them girls, as pretty as you are."

"What do I gotta do, just come out here and put on a sexy outfit?"

"Naw, it's a lot more complicated. It would take me weeks to explain everything to you. You have to have representation, someone that knows the people out here, else those guys over there you saw me talking to will beat you up real bad. They serious 'bout their bread. Those streets belong to them."

"You know them," Linda said, just as I hoped she would. "You could represent me."

"Naw, I don't know. It's a rough game."

"Please. I could handle myself out there better than any of those bitches."

"Well… Are you sure that's something you wanna do?"

"Yeah. Can we, can we?" she begged, like a kid asking for a new toy.

"All right. When do you wanna start?"

"Tomorrow night," she answered confidently.

"OK, we'll do it," I said, looking out my window with a smile.

And for the next 20 years that's what I did with my life. I pimped hoes for a living. The first 10 years were a decent ride, but as I got older and wiser it became just another job that wasn't for me.

Chapter 10

After a hard day's hustle on the Ave I came home to find Linda dressed and ready to start her new career.

"Take me to the shelter so I can get the rest of my clothes, then we'll go to the city," she said before I could even take off my jacket. I could tell she'd been thinking about her new venture all day.

We went to the shelter, and she was in and out of the building in less than 10 minutes. I helped her carry her two large black plastic bags filled with clothes to the car. She got dressed on our way to the track. By the time we got there she looked like a star. On the way I explained the business to her.

"But it doesn't seem fair that I should have to give you all of my money," she protested.

"I agree with you, Linda, but that's how this game is played. Remember, it was you who wanted to play."

"What do I get in return?" she asked.

"You're already getting it. You have a safe place to lay your head, a real home, and it's yours, not your abusive foster parents or the city's. As long as we're partners we share and trust each other. So when you hand me money and I put it in my pocket it's not mine just because I'm managing it. It's ours."

"That's what you say now, but we just met. How I know you not gonna take all the money and leave me?"

I pulled over. "I told you this job wasn't for you," I sighed, making a U turn and started to head back towards Bedford Stuyvesant. "I'm takin' you back."

"No, I'm sorry. I'll give it a try. Turn back around."

"You sure?" I asked as I pulled over again.

"I'm sure. Let's do it."

I made another U turn and headed back toward Manhattan.

****

It was Friday night. Tricks were tricking and hoes were hoeing. I pulled up to House Man on 43rd Street, got out, and greeted him. "What the deal, House Man?"

House Man was a smooth, slick-talking pimp. He stood about 7'2" and weighed about 300 pounds. House Man kept his head clean shaven and sported a well-kept goatee. He always wore expensive sweatsuits and brand new white sneakers. House Man loved basketball. He used to be a college basketball player for Rutgers University. House was offered a contract to play for the New York Knicks, but he met a street girl who knocked him off his feet and taught him the game. House Man chose the streets over basketball, but he always talked about his college years and where he would have been if he'd gone pro.

"Cash is in the back. Probably sleepin' in the car," House Man told me, pointing to the parking lot.

I walked over to the back of the parking lot, knocked on the window, and yelled, "Cash, wake up man! Let me in!"

I knocked several times until I woke him. He unlocked the doors, and I got in the driver's side. "Man I done come up," I said.

"Oh, you done knocked a bitch huh? Who, that little fine red bitch over there?"

"Yeah," I replied.

"That's money right there! You 'bout to get paid, baby boy. You gonna need a shopping bag to carry all that money by morning! You'll have a stack

twenties that could choke a dinosaur. This calls for a

celebration, man! Let's go get a blast."

"Cool," I replied, starting the car.

"Just a minute, Rick, let me break my bitch."

Cash got out and walked toward Pleasure.

SMACK, SMACK. Cash was beating Pleasure.

She screamed and tried to block her face, but Cash was

too fast. Each blow landed on her cheek. Cashmere

suddenly stopped hitting the girl and yelled, "Bitch, I'm

tired of hurting my precious hands on you. Smack

yourself, bitch."

She looked at him as if he was crazy. "What?"

"You heard what the fuck I said. Unless you

want me to do it," Cashmere yelled. He raised his hand

as if he was going to smack her again.

"OK!" Pleasure screamed.

She began hitting herself. *SMACK, SMACK, SMACK* I heard coming from Pleasure as she viciously punished and humiliated herself.

"That's not hard enough, bitch. Don't make me do it!" Cashmere threatened as he walked back to the car, lighting a joint on the way.

Cash got back in the car and rudely shouted, "155th and 8th!"

The address was a little candy store just across the street from the Polar Ground Housing Projects in Harlem where we bought our coke from.

As I drove towards the exit of the parking lot Pleasure was still smacking herself repeatedly. Cash put his widow down and yelled, "Stop! Now go and get my bread, maggot!"

"What's up, playboy?" I asked casually, in an attempt to find out why he treated her the way he did.

He quickly snapped at me, "A playboy is a trick; I'm a pimp!"

There was a short silence that made me feel uneasy.

"Sorry to come down on you like that, Rick," Cash broke the silence. "Ain't your fault the punk bitch money lookin' funny."

"Man, I ain't sweatin' that," I replied, even though I knew he owed me an apology.

I was ashamed of Cashmere. I was ashamed of myself for not helping Pleasure. I thought it best to mind my business regardless of what I was feeling. I felt sorry for Pleasure. I thought, *why doesn't she just leave him? She has every opportunity to leave when she gets in a trick's car.*

My mom instilled good moral values in me, and the business went against some of the things that I learned growing up. Dad taught me that hitting women was OK, but I knew that Dad was wrong.

I opened the window, changed the radio station several times, and stared out of the driver's side window at each red light. I couldn't look at Cash. There was an uncomfortable silence as I fell into deep thought. Cash knew I was irritated; my body language gave me away. He was good at reading people.

Cash finally explained further, "There is no right or wrong way to pimp, although there are rules that we need to follow, as in every game. As you grow in the game you'll develop your own style. If you handle a situation differently than me it doesn't make you wrong. Emotions are something that will hinder your ability to pimp effectively if you can't control them. You have to be able to control your emotions if you want to control a woman's emotions. Remember: it's about funds, not feelings."

I pushed the incident as far back in my mind as possible and tried to act like it didn't happen. I knew that if Linda saw Cashmere's behavior I would lose her for sure.

Cash changed the subject. "Man, now that you're pimpin' you need a catchy pimp name." He thought for a few seconds. "Slick, Slick Rick. I'm gonna call you Slick," he said, and he did from then on.

I parked about a block away from the coke spot, and Cash got out of the car and went into the store. He stayed in there for about five minutes, then came out with a small brown paper bag in his hand. Pop always made sure we left the spot with a bag in our hand. It just looked better if the store was being watched by the police.

I drove back to the track while Cash rolled a coke cigarette. I looked in the rear view mirror and my heart skipped a beat. I said in a sharp voice, "Keep it down. Five O followin' us."

Cash glanced in the mirror. "Just be cool. Bend on Lenox Ave." I turned on Lenox. The cop car turned behind us. We were definitely being followed.

Cash stashed the coke, moving slow and easy so the cops wouldn't see as he slipped the package down the front of his pants. At the same time, he pulled out a nickel-plated 9mm and slid it under his left leg. I could see the black handle protrude from between the leather seat and his leg.

"What the fuck is the ratchet for?" I snarled. I stared at the handle of the gun. Everything was happening way too fast. I wanted to explain to Cash that the situation wasn't serious enough for a gun, but there was no time.

"Just be cool, Slick, I got this," he replied calmly, as if he'd been in that situation a hundred times before.

By the time we got to the middle of the block, flashing red and blue lights had lit up the street. My mind raced, but each minute seemed like an hour. My heart pounded, my breath came heavily, as I passed gas uncontrollably. As we pulled our car over, I knew I was about to be caught in the middle of a shoot-out. One that we couldn't possibly win.

The cops walked up to the car, one on the left and one on the right. Both of them shined their bright flashlights at us, nearly blinding me. They were two nasty white cops who probably hated blacks. The one on the driver's side walked up to me and said, "License, registration, and insurance card" as he shinned the flashlight on the registration sticker. The other walked up to Cash and shined his flashlight in Cash's face.

107

As Cash reached for the glove compartment I glanced over at him. Cash was cool as a fan. He handed me the paperwork and put his left hand on the seat about 2 inches away from the gun. How the officer on the driver's side didn't see it is beyond me. Knowing that I'd be the only unarmed person involved in the shoot-out just made matters worse. There was nothing I could do at that point but hope to start the engine and peel out of there as fast as I could once I heard the first shot. In less than a minute there was going to be a hail of gun fire.

"Where are you guys coming from?" the officer on the driver's side asked me.

"A friend's house," I lied, knowing the officer probably saw Cash go in to the spot. They'd probably been watching the spot the whole time.

I thought, *This can't be happening. I'm getting out of this somehow. I'm not going to die like this.*

I heard the cops' radios cackle, "211 in progress, 147th and Lenox." The cop on my side said something to his partner, looked at me, and said, "Consider this your lucky day." They both ran back to their cruiser and sped off down Lenox Ave.

"Ooohwee! The pimp god is with them fools tonight!" Cash crowed as we drove away. "I didn't have to smoke their punk asses. They oughta consider themselves lucky. Man, this calls for a blast!"

Cash pulled the package of coke from his pants and scooped the shiny, glistening white powder with his long pinky fingernail. I could see the reflection of the 2 karat diamond ring he wore on the dashboard every time his hand went up or down.

Cash carried on discussing what he would have done to the cops, but I kept silent. I knew if I spoke I would only reveal how scared I had been. I had nearly shit myself. I thought of the story Cash told me about the dope boy he killed in Marcy Projects. When he told me I thought he was full of shit, but after seeing the way he handled that situation, I quickly became a believer. Cashmere was a cold-blooded murderer.

He put the gun back in his waistband and put a cassette tape in the tape deck.

****

"Bend the track a few times, Slick," he said in his cool Barry White voice.

We bent the track, blasting "Too Short" through his new Bose speakers, hollering at hoes and snorting coke. When I finally parked on the track Blue walked over to the car and got in.

"Dig, Pimpin', the Muslims just had some words with us. They said they gonna build a mosque across the street and want us to move our business elsewhere."

Cash took offense, as I knew he would. Blue knew it to, which was why he made it a point to tell Cash.

"I ain't going nowhere," Cash replied. "This is my home, and I ain't gonna let anybody push me out of it. Where these cats at? I wanna talk to 'em."

"They just pulled off in a white Ford," Blue answered.

I quickly changed the subject. I wanted to keep Cash calm and spoil Blue's plan. Blue wanted a war, and Cash was just the guy to start one.

At that moment Pleasure got out of a trick's car, just close enough for Cash to see her. She stopped about two cars away, knowing better than to walk up on a car full of pimps. Cash passed me the coke and excused himself. He walked over to Pleasure, and she handed him something without a word. He returned to the car, and she walked back down the street, switching her fine black ass and smiling and waving at cars.

When Cash got back in the car I told him, "Play that shit 'Bitches Ain't Nothin' But Hoes and Tricks'." He blasted the track and forgot all about what Blue was talking about. I think Blue did too, considering that he had the bill filled with cocaine in his hand by the time Cash got back to the car.

I'd never ask a man how much his women gave him. I felt that was personal and not my business. I guessed Cash was having a good night, though, because he chose to tell me.

"$345! Not bad, and it's just after 2am. Dig, Slick: that bitch is stashin' my bread. Let me tell you how I know. A bitch not gonna come back with an odd number like $345. No one is gonna give her $45 or $15. It should be $40 or $50, so she should have given me $340 or $350. Strictly pimp talk, Pimpin'. Never tell a dirty maggot bitch anything like what I just told you, 'cause as soon as they know you're hip they'll change the game. Never let the right hand know what the left one is doing. Bitch think I'm stupid. She think she's pulling one over on me. I've suspected the bitch of stashing my bread for a couple of weeks now. I always follow my gut."

The sun started coming up. All the pimps and hoes were still out snorting coke and telling stories. The trick traffic died down, and the hoes stood around looking worn out.

I turned to Cash and said, "Looks like it's over, Pimpin'."

"Yeah I'm hip, but I'm gonna keep my bitches out for at least another hour, just to be a ball buster," he chuckled.

"I'm out. Tomorrow is another day," I said as I slapped him five.

I could tell he wanted me to stay so he could continue teaching Pimping 101, but I walked back to my car and tapped the horn for Linda to get in. She came to the car smiling.

"Daddy, I ran circles around them hoes," she bragged. "Tricks are still riding around the track lookin' for me."

Linda's first night out she made over $500. It was obvious that she loved her new job. I had never made that amount of money in such a short period of time in my life. The feeling was like a natural high Every time Linda handed me money it felt as though I'd taken a fix. I used to get the same felling every Friday night when my supervisor handed me my check—only now I was being paid much more money much faster.

Chapter 11

Within two months I'd molded Linda into the type of women I wanted, and I was also molded into a full-fledged pimp. Any time there was something I didn't understand I'd ask Cash, and he'd explain it to me or give me advice.

Every morning Linda went to sleep around 6 am and woke up in the evening. When she woke up she went out shopping for a new outfit, got her nails done, or whatever else she found to spend money on. She became a spoiled brat, but we both had everything we could ask for. Within six months I had approximately $10,000 stacked up, my car was paid for, I'd moved to a bigger apartment in a better neighborhood, and I had quit wholesaling.

The game was good, but I felt that Linda was becoming too attached to me. She started acting like she was my girlfriend. We argued a lot, and she even threatened to leave me. Cashmere informed me on how to handle the situation. He told me, "Once a bitch becomes comfortable being your only bitch she's gonna get outta pocket. She gonna start doing all kind of underhanded shit just because she knows she can get away with it. If she knows she's your only source of income she got you; you don't have her. Man, Slick, you gotta find another ho, one ho too close to no ho. Now peep game, Pimpin'; write a letter and mail it to yourself. Address it to come from any bitch's name. You want it to say something like, 'Daddy, I missed you so much and if things don't work out between you and that mud duck bitch, jus' say the word and I'll be there in 2 shakes. Daddy, you my king and I'm always down for your crown. I'll wire you some more money tonight' and whoopdie whoo, whoopdie whoo. Put it in your own words. You know the things to say to strike your bitch's nerve. Keep the letter in the envelope and put it somewhere you know she's gonna see it, and the bitch gonna read it, guaranteed. Then she'll know she's replaceable, and she'll stop actin' the fool. That'll buy you enough time to catch another bitch."

I did what Cash said, and it worked like a charm. Linda found the letter on the dresser, and when I walked in the house she had it in her hand. Her face was red as a beet.

"Daddy, who's Barbra, and who the fuck she callin' a mud duck?" Linda yelled.

I snatched the letter from her. "Whatchu readin' my mail for?" I asked, trying to sound like I was mad at her. "Barbra your replacement if you keep doin' stupid shit like that."

Tears began to roll down Linda's cheeks. "Daddy, you gonna replace me?"

"Well, I've been thinkin' 'bout it," I said casually while walking towards the bedroom to lay down for a short nap before work.

I smiled because I executed a well thought-out plan. *Cool,* I thought, *I am pretty good at this. I can control a woman's mind.* Then I heard Linda sobbing in the living room, and my smile began to fade. I lay awake for a little while listening to Linda's sobs, trying to fight the temptation to console her. I told myself, *Ignore her. Linda needs to get used to it. This is how the game is played.* I thought, *how can she be so possessive anyway? She doesn't even like men. Linda knows I have to share myself too. She's not a turn out anymore; she's a seasoned ho.* A turn out is a term we use for someone that's new to the game.

I must have slept for an hour before I felt a tap on my shoulder. "Daddy, can we talk?" Linda asked, sitting on the edge of the bed.

118

"What do you wanna talk about?"

"Daddy, please don't fire me. I'll straighten up, I promise," Linda cried.

"Lin, all the bickerin' gotta stop. When I tell you to do something, my word is law. I'm the star of the show."

"I'm sorry, Daddy, I'll stay in pocket," Linda replied.

"You know how to play chess?" Linda nodded tearfully. "Well chess is a lot like the game. We have the pawns, the knights, the rooks, and the bishops that we move around when we're out there. You are the queen, the strongest piece on the board, and I am the king. My movement is very limited. Everybody has to come together for one common cause, and that is to make sure the king makes it to the other side rich, without being captured. If you don't make the right moves, the moves that I instruct you to make, you leave the king open to being captured. And what happens when the king is captured?"

"Game over," Linda answered. "Daddy, I've never had anyone that was really on my side, a partner. You are all I got, Daddy, and the last thing I need is for you to leave me. I'll do anything but please don't leave me, Daddy. I'm sorry I'm so possessive. I'll play my position. I don't even mind handing all of my money over to you. Please just don't leave me."

Once I felt Linda's pain I got serious. I didn't want to game or con her; I really felt for her. I sat up on the bed and gave Linda a caring hug. I held her while she cried. I felt her chest heave as she tried to catch her breath.

I wore many hats, and at times I'd have to quickly change my job description. I'd have to go from lover to psychiatrist, teacher, or father figure, sometimes within seconds. Whatever my women needed I had to accommodate. It was hard, tiresome work, but it was essential to my business. I quickly changed my job description to a compassionate, understanding, caring person. When it was about something that I believed in or if the person was someone I really wanted to help, I gave of myself with ease. Even though I tried to hide my emotions, sometimes I couldn't. Knowing what Linda had been through made me feel genuine compassion. Even though I wanted my business to run smoothly, I did not want Linda to hurt.

"Baby, I'm not gonna leave you," I cooed. "It's me and you against the world. You don't have to worry, I promise you I'm never gonna leave you."

Linda held me tighter. I felt her body trembling, so I continued holding her until she got it all out and was ready to let go.

Chapter 12

Despite my emotions going astray I put my business first. It was time for some fresh game, so I went to Midtown to recruit. While driving up 8th Ave I saw a pretty, fat Spanish broad. She had sky blue eyes and long brown hair with natural blonde streaks in it. Her breast and legs were huge, and she had a smile that could brighten anyone's day.

I yelled, "Can a gentleman give you a lift?" as I pulled over. She got in, and we drove around and talked for about an hour.

I always took my prospects out of their environment because I knew I'd have a better chance at keeping them off balance. As long as she was off balance I would be in control, so I headed for the Queensboro Bridge, never once asking her where she was headed.

"What's your name?" I asked.

"Serena."

"What's your vice, Serena?"

"I'm a sucker for handsome black men."

I smiled. "Where do you live?"

"Uptown on Edgecombe Ave," Serena replied.

I flirted with her because I knew that she probably didn't get too many passes because of her weight. "What a man gotta do to have a pretty woman like you?"

She blushed, just as I expected she would.

I kept pouring it on. "I know we just met but I've seen you on the track before. Please forgive me if I don't sound like a gentleman, but I have to say it. Every time I see you my nuts just be doin' the happy dance."

She smiled again. I put my hand on my forehead, trying to look embarrassed. "I apologize, I shouldn't have said that. I was way outta pocket." I hung my head.

"No it's OK," Serena replied. "I wish my man would look at me like that. He act like he doesn't want me."

I could tell she really liked what I was saying, because she couldn't stop smiling. "Maybe one day you will accept me as your man," I continued.

"Maybe," she responded.

"There's another track out in Jamaica, Queens, and the paper real long out there." I figured I might as well get to the point. We were already in Long Island City, Queens.

"Where?"

"Off Hillside Avenue."

"Can you take me there?"

"Sure, I'll take you now. But you know it's pimpin' goin' on, right?"

"It ain't hard to tell. Shit, I need some pimpin'
in my life," Serena said as she looked in the mirror and
combed her pretty hair.

"Cool," I said. It was just what I needed to hear.
This was almost too easy.

When we got to 161st Street and 89th Avenue in
Jamaica it was about 5pm. Kind of early but I figured
what the hell, I better seize the moment. There was still
some pretty good after-work trick traffic at that time of
day, so I threw the dice. I dropped her off around the
corner from the Bristle Hotel, a little red and white
hotel on 89th Ave that was known for prostitution and
drug activity. As soon as I let her out of the car I saw
the car behind me pick her up in my rear view mirror.

Serena made $240 in two hours.

I was tired because I hadn't slept yet that day, so
I figured I would save her for the night traffic; besides,
I wasn't hurting for money. If she got away at least I

125

would've made a profit. I tapped the horn twice, and Serena walked to the car.

"I'll accept this $240 as a down payment on your chosen fee," I said as I added $170 to my already huge bank roll. I separated $70 and handed it to Serena. "Go pick up an outfit for tonight."

I drove her home, dropped her off, and told her to be ready at 11pm. When she got out of the car she turned and shouted, "I'll call you 'bout 9."

Chapter 13

I dropped Linda off on 44th Street and 11th Ave at about 10pm and drove uptown to get Serena. On my way there I got a call from her.

"Daddy I'm sorry, I overslept. That's why I didn't call earlier."

I didn't care but I fussed about it anyway. "When you say you're gonna do something I expect it to be done."

"Sorry, Daddy. Please forgive me?" she whined, her voice cracking as if she really did just wake up.

"Be dressed in 15 minutes."

I knew it would be at least an hour before I got there, but I wanted to make sure she'd be ready.

I called Serena as I was approaching the 125th Street exit of the FDR Drive. When I got to her building she was downstairs waiting. Serena got in the car, and the first thing I did was compliment her on her shoes to set the tone. I kept pouring it on for about 15 minutes. She loved it.

I pulled over and got out of the car to go to a Chinese grocery store on 47th Street and 11th Ave. I bought two boxes of condoms and a pretty red rose. I knew the rose would help strengthen my game. I always liked to have a woman in a good mood just before they went to work.

As I walked back to the car she wasn't paying attention to me, so when I handed her the rose it was a surprise. "When I saw it I immediately started thinking 'bout you. Isn't it pretty?" I gave her some game along with the rose.

"Awww, it is," she replied as if she was going to cry.

I gently put my hand under her chin and held her jaw with my forefinger and thumb. I turned her face in my direction so she could see the sincerity in my eyes as I spoke in a smooth, low tone. "You're much prettier than that rose."

She gleefully smiled from ear to ear and batted her sparkling blue eyes before reaching over to give me a warm, pleasant hug. Most overweight women are insecure because of their weight. They don't get many complements. But compliments make people feel good, and it's natural for a person to want to be with someone who makes them feel good. The compliments, roses, and nice statements were just my way of fishing around for the right keys to strengthen the contract. I knew it was going to be a good night.

As we approached the track I saw the streets filled with ladies of the night. The trick traffic was thick. I handed Serena the condoms and said, "Go suck up all the butter in the gutter." She got out of the car with a big pretty smile on her face and walked up the street switching her oversized ass. Linda saw her get out of the car and immediately stormed over to me. She was furious. Her nostrils flared, her eyes were piercing, and tiny beads of sweat hung on her nose. She was breathing heavy and her face was tense as she bit her bottom lip.

I thought, *Here we go again with this bullshit.* I took a deep breath, then released a distressed sigh.

"Daddy, who's that bitch?" she yelled.

"That's your new wife in law."

"Wife in law? Why? Don't I make enough money?"

Linda standing on the corner of the Ho Stroll yelling at me didn't look good. I looked at the street, where cars were slowing down to watch the commotion. Linda was in such a rage that she didn't even notice the scene she was causing. It looked as though I'd assaulted her, and I would have a lot of explaining to do if the police rode by. I had to do something quick.

Once she finished yelling I explained in a comforting voice, "You know what a kind-hearted man I am. The poor girl needs my guidance. She's a good money-catcher, and she's just here for a lil while. Just until I can buy you that car I've been promising you."

Linda began to calm down. She wiped her tears with her forefinger.

"OK, Daddy," she said softly. "You the boss."

A mixture of tears and mascara still ran down her cheeks as she put her hand in her bra to pull out $150. She handed it to me, then walked up the street looking both satisfied and confused.

The bickering and arguments that I got from every one of the women that stayed for a considerable amount of time became extremely annoying. I had well over a hundred women in my career. At times I just wanted to walk away from them and never return, but my money was at stake and I was so money hungry. I'd come to the conclusion that Linda was never going to overcome her possessive behavior, but she was such a good person and a hard worker that she deserved the car I promised her, so right there I made a decision that I was going to keep my end of the deal.

****

An hour went by, but there was no sign of Serena. Two hours went by—no sign of her. Finally, a dark blue pickup truck pulled over in the middle of the block. Serena got out and walked over to me with a hundred dollar bill in her hand.

"Baby girl listen," I said. "A hundred dollars for two hours just ain't cuttin' it. Timin' is everything in this business. Work on your timin'. Practice the 3 G's: get in, get it, and get out. No small talk, no bullshitin'."

"OK Daddy, I'm sorry," she replied in a low voice. She knew she was wrong.

Serena caught three or four more dates that night. By the time the sun was coming up she handed me $550. Serena was paying like she weighed.

****

We left the track at about 6:30 that morning. As we drove down Hillside Avenue trying to decide what we were going to eat I saw a look of disappointment on Linda's face. "Sorry Daddy, I know I didn't do too well last night," she said while reaching in her stocking for the last hundred dollars she had. The last thing Linda wanted was for Serena to make more money than her.

"Chicken one day, feathers the next," I replied to make her feel better.

I think Serena knew that she made the most money, so she took advantage of her position. "Daddy, can you sleep at my house today?" she asked while holding her pretty red rose for Linda to see.

I looked over at Linda. If looks could kill Linda would have been wanted for murder.

"Sure, I'll sleep over if you promise to respect me in the morning," I replied jokingly.

Competition always brought out the best in my women. I loved it because no matter who lost, I always won.

I dropped Linda off and took Serena to her small one bedroom apartment in Harlem. When we walked into Serena's apartment the walls were painted a pale yellow, an exact match of the yellow linoleum tiles on the floor. The kitchen was at the point of entry. The sink and stove were to the front left of me, and a refrigerator was in the front right corner. There was a dirty white door directly in front of me. That was her bedroom.

Serena wanted to have sex with me, but I didn't know how I was going pull it off. The only thing that got me through those unforgettable, unpleasant sex acts was thinking about the money she had the potential to make—that and Janet Jackson. Over time I'd become just like the girls when it came to sex: I had sex when I knew I would be paid for it. I had sex with maybe 20 percent of the women I had. The ones whom I had sex with usually had low self-esteem, and I slept with them because they needed a little more from me than just game. I have never been attracted to overweight women, so I psyched myself into believing I was having sex with Janet Jackson when I slept with Serena. I always used Janet in that situation. Serena needed to know that I thought she was attractive enough to have sex with. Usually money motivated me to sleep with my women, but not all the time: there were also some women to whom I was really attracted. For some reason

135

acting came natural to me, so I knew how to fake enjoying sex to make my partner happy. But there were times when even Janet couldn't help me. In those situations I just ended up embarrassed because my body would not listen to my brain.

Every time I thought about money and Janet I pushed harder until her body began shaking uncontrollably. At that point I knew she was finished. Thank God because Lord knows I didn't want any more of her fat ass.

Serena quickly fell asleep, so I knew my job was done. I dozed off.

Serena didn't have a hardship story, and from the information I gathered she was just out to have fun. I'd had plenty of women like her. I didn't have the same compassionate, remorseful, sorry feelings for women like Serena that I had for other girls. Each woman had a unique story, and I dealt with each accordingly.

****

I was rudely awakened by a short, heavy-set West Indian man in a black two piece jean suit. He had a butcher knife in one hand and a bottle of Jack Daniels Black Label in the other. He was angry, and his eyes were blood red. He looked down on me screaming, "Get yer ass outa my house!!"

I was nervous, and my heart was pounding. I looked around for a weapon, but I couldn't find one. I moved quickly, reaching for my pants while I was talking to him trying to calm him down. My tongue was my only weapon, but it didn't seem to be working.

"Hey man, I'm sorry, I didn't know she was your woman. Please put the knife down."

"Well you don't fuck me as good as him!" Serena shouted.

It didn't help the situation. Was Serena trying to get me killed? The man came towards me with a look of death in his eyes. I knew I didn't have enough time to finished getting dressed. There was only two ways out of that small bedroom: I could fight with a knife-wielding drunk man or jump out the window.

I went for the window.

Good thing we were on the second floor. As I went through the window, badly bruising my back from the chipped paint, I could hear him right behind me. There were bushes directly underneath me that cut my face and legs when I landed. After climbing out of the bushes I finished putting my pants on. Leaves and twigs stuck to my body, and I noticed that it was raining. I stood in the grass soaked and wet with no shirt on, no socks, and one shoe in my hand. Passersby stared and whispered. The feeling of humiliation was overwhelming. I quickly ran to my car and drove home, feeling like an ass.

When I got home I called Linda and told her to bring some clothes down for me.

"What?" she asked.

"Just do it!" I screamed in response.

When she got downstairs to the car she couldn't believe her eyes. "What happened to you?" she asked.

I ignored her, snatched the clothes, and got dressed. She struggled to hold back her laughter, but ultimately failed. After laughing for about an hour, she helped me patch up my wounds from my fall into the bushes.

"You wanted to go with that fat bitch, huh?" she chuckled. "Bet you'll stay your ass home now."

Chapter 14

"What the fuck happened to you? You have a fight with your cat?" Cashmere teased me.

I explained what happened to Cash, and he suggested we take a ride uptown to pay Serena and her man a visit.

We drove uptown and parked the Caddy about two blocks away from Serena's building. Before we got out of the car Cash slid the top of his 9mm back, putting a bullet in the chamber.

"Is that really necessary?" I asked.

"Man, we gotta address that shit. If pimps find out that shit went down and you didn't address it pimps will be kidnapping your hoes every night." He rambled on, and the more he spoke the more I began to see things his way. There was nothing soft about me. I was not going to let anyone do that o me without a repercussion.

The lobby door was locked, so Cash went through the adjacent building, crossed the roof, and came down to let me in. Just before we got to the apartment Cash whispered, "When someone comes to the door tell them they dropped a piece of mail in front your door and you're returning it. Don't show your face."

I knocked on the door and stood to the left side, out of view. Cash stood to the right with his hand on the handle of his gun, ready to rush the door when it opened.

The anticipation made my heart beat faster and harder. I felt butterflies in my stomach because I knew that as soon as the door opened there was no turning back.

No one came. Cash put his ear to the door to listen for noise inside.

"Knock again," he whispered.

I knocked again, a little harder. Cash put his ear to the door to listen again; no answer. I banged on the door a few times.

We left without accomplishing our mission.

****

On the way back to the track Cash begin teaching. "Let this be a lesson to you, Slick. The next time you knock a bitch find out everything you can 'bout her first. There's obviously a lot of things you didn't know 'bout the bitch. You never walk in a bitch's house unless you are absolutely sure there is no man involved. Just imagine if you had caught a dude in *your* house. Most important, Slick, never fall asleep in a bitch's house. Dude could've killed you and he had every right to. You my brother, and that's why I'm givin' it to you straight from the hip. In a lot of ways you're wrong, but I'm gonna stand by you. You shouldn't have fucked the bitch. That may be all she wanted. A bitch need to believe that you are different, Slick. Most bitches can find a dick anywhere. They get passes all day, they can't even walk to the store without some lame-ass tryin' to fuck 'em. When you show a bitch that you're not interested in her body she's gonna be curious 'bout you. She'll be more interested in you, especially if she's a fine motherfucker and she knows it."

I thought Cash would never stop. I sat there as if I was in grade school listening to my teacher.

Cash continued, "Slick, I can chop my dick off and still pimp 'cause I give a bitch eargasms all day. I'm not sayin' never fuck your bitch, cause if you don't who you gonna fuck? A square? That's disrespectful to the game. I'm saying you have to be a higher-paid

143

prostitute then she is. Dig, Pimpin': a bitch of mine may get $60 for a blow and $100 for sex, but I'm gonna break her ass for at least $10,000 before I fuck her, no matter how fine she is."

I was sick of listening to my brother's bullshit, so I called it an early night, slapped Cash five, and walked to my car.

We didn't accomplish the mission of giving Serena some payback, but I looked at the bright side. I got close to $800 for my trouble.

Chapter 15

I was startled by my ringing cell phone. I didn't recognize the number. When I finally answered, a voice on the other end said, "You forgot about me."

I replied, "Naw, I ain't forget 'bout you, what's up witcha?" I tried to figure out who it was.

"I had a fight with my boyfriend. He kicked me out."

"Do you want me to pick you up?"

"Yeah."

"Where you at?"

"Remember where you dropped me off on Brevoort?"

When she told me where she was I instantly remembered who she was. Slim. I didn't think she would call.

Slim was a pretty little dark-skinned girl with brown bedroom eyes. Her hair was a mess when I met her. She stood about 5'5" and weighed about 110 pounds. Her clothes were old and worn out, so I knew she could use a little help. She was very loud, and her voice was squeaky and irritating.

"I can swing by and get you as soon as I wake up. I'm 'bout to take it down right now."

"You promise? I don't have any place else to go."

"You got my word."

When I hung up Linda said, "Sound like you done come up."

"Yeah, seems that way," I replied as I fell back to sleep.

That night before work I went to Brevoort Ave to pick Slim up at an old nasty crack house belonging to Tim. I knew Tim from when I used to live in that neighborhood. He had dreads, not because he wanted them but because he never washed or combed his hair. He always reeked with body odor, and his house smelled like shit. Tim had one leg; I never asked what happened to the other. Tim usually had some kind of homeless woman lying around his house. I used to go over occasionally to look for new prospects.

I knocked on the door, and I heard a squeaky voice come from inside.

"Who is it?"

"Slick."

Slim opened the door. To my surprise she didn't look bad in her black spandex halter top and 6 inch heels. I wouldn't even have to take her shopping.

"You comin' in?" Slim asked.

I took my last deep breath of fresh air before walking in.

"What's the deal, Tim?" I shouted as I walked toward the back of the small studio apartment. Tim stuck his hand out for me to shake it and I did.

"Long time no see, Pimpin'," Tim said as he stood up on his one leg and balanced himself on the brown recliner that was in the middle of the floor.

"Yeah, I've been a little busy."

"Y'all know each other?" Slim interrupted.

Tim replied happily, "I've known Pimpin' fo years. He cool; you'll be OK wit' him." Tim was marketing me. That was cool, even though I knew it would cost me few dollars before I walked out of the door.

After talking to Tim for about 5 minutes I yelled, "What da deal, Slim, you still getting down wit' me or what?"

Slim replied, "Yeah, I am, but I'm busy right now," as she lifted the stem to her face to take another dose of the potent crack cocaine she was smoking.

I sat there for a few minutes talking to Tim and thinking of a way to get Slim out of there. I knew from experimenting with crack when I hung out with Mel that she wasn't going anywhere until it was all gone. She only had two small rocks left. After the rocks are gone people tend to want more, and they will do just about anything to get it. She finally finished about 45 minutes later. I could tell she wanted more because she was on the floor looking for leftovers.

"Grab your purse," I said. "We'll get a few rocks on our way to your new home."

I gave Tim $10 and was out of there in less than 5 minutes. We stopped at the crack house on Madison Street and Franklin Avenue to pick up 3 more rocks. When I handed her the rocks she looked depressed.

"I'm going to rehab this week," she said. "I had enough of this."

"Wise choice Baby Girl. If you're serious I'll help you find one, but you have to initiate that move."

Drug addicts always talked about how they were going to rehab, but they very rarely made it there. It was usually all talk, so I didn't want to waste my time.

"So what did Nick teach you 'bout the game?" I asked her.

"Just to give his punk ass the money," she replied.

"Well, Slim, here's the deal: you're under new management now. I'm only here to manage your money and make sure you are living better; that's what I get paid for. Although things will be done my way your opinion counts, and it's very important to me."

Slim looked at me in a strange way, almost as if I'd said something wrong. "Nick used to just tell me what to do. If I didn't do it he'd go upside my head. He said he was there to protect me, and I'd never make it out there without him."

I replied, "Well, like I said, you're under new management. I'm gonna keep it real wit' you. The truth is that a pimp can only provide you with a little protection. When you're in a car with a trick it's just you and him; your pimp is nowhere around. You have to protect yourself. When you're walking the track and the police ride up on you and ask who your pimp is you're better off saying you don't have one, 'cause they'll lock your ass up faster if you say you do. My name will only protect you by representing you on the fast track among others that's in the life. Furthermore, I'll never put my hands on you. I will sever our relationship before I do that."

Slim raised her eyebrows and looked at me. "Thanks for keeping it real with me, but why are you telling me this?" she asked.

"I feel it's important that we understand exactly what we're getting into before we make a major business move like the one we're about to make. Are you sure this is something you wanna do? If not, I'll understand, and we'll part here with no hard feelings."

"I've heard 'bout you," Slim said. "I heard you're a real good guy to work for. You got a bitch named Linda, right?"

"Yeah, Linda is with me, she good people too."

"Linda and I went on a double date once at the Marriott Hotel on Broadway and 44th. The trick was into some weird S&M shit. He wanted us to humiliate him and kick his ass. I couldn't do it but Linda had no problem. She spit in his face, pushed him on the bed, and beat the shit outa him. The trick was screaming,

'Please Mistress Linda, I'm, sorry I've been a bad boy!' She was really enjoying it. I got scared because the trick was screaming so loud, so I left. The next day Linda came down to the renegade track, found me, and gave me $200. She said if it wasn't for me she wouldn't have got the date, and I at least deserve that."

I couldn't help but laugh. "Yeah, that's my girl. Sounds like something she'd do. She hates men and she has a lot of integrity."

I dropped Slim off at the Days Inn in Bay Ridge, Brooklyn, and told her that she'd only be there for a couple of days before I found her an apartment. I could have taken her home with me and Linda but I didn't want the drugs around me. Crack heads were normally messy and careless. They lost paraphernalia and didn't care about cleaning. I didn't mind putting up with it every once in a while, but I couldn't live with it.

****

I explained to Linda that she had a new wife in law so it wouldn't come as a surprise.

"Long as she knows her place," Linda said when I told her. "That bitch ain't sittin' in my seat."

"No, Lin, she'll be in the back." I never understood the big deal about a seat. "I'm goin' to pick her up now. Be back in a half hour."

Even though I knew Slim would be awake because of the coke she was smoking I called the room 10 minutes before I got there. Her clothes were on and she was ready to go when I arrived.

"Shake a tail feather Slim!" I yelled.

"Can I take one more hit?"

"Hurry up, I'm tryin' to get the hell outa here, I'm putting the pedal to the metal tonight."

I watched as Slim put the long glass stem filled with cocaine residue in her mouth and lit it like a cigarette. She took a long puff, held it in, then ran to the

154

window to let it out. She started breathing heavy and looking around on the floor as if she dropped something. Then she stopped and just stood there with the stem and lighter in her hand like a statue.

"Slim you stuck?" I asked.

"Yeah," she whispered back.

"You better shake that shit. I ain't got time for this."

She wouldn't budge. I had to snatch the stem and lighter from her, grab her hand, and lead her to the door. When I got her to the door she held on to the knob.

"No I can't go," she whispered. Then she looked back and screamed, "WHO'S THAT?!?"

My heart skipped a beat. I looked behind me. No one was there.

"AHHH, YOU SAW THEM?!?" Slim screamed again.

"Saw who, Slim?"

She started whispering again. "They coming, they coming through the window, you see them?"

Suddenly she took off. She ran down the stairs screaming, "DON'T LET 'EM GET ME, DON'T LET 'EM GET ME!!"

I ran after her. I caught her pulled her close to me, holding her tight until she calmed down. She was shaking as if she was terrified. After she calmed down a little I managed to get her into the car. I drove to the nearest liquor store and bought her a half pint of Bacardi Dark because I knew that the alcohol was a downer and would bring her back to normal. I had to argue with her to get her to drink it. After she drank about a quarter of the bottle she began to calm down.

"I'm sorry," she said. "I get if you don't want me no more."

"I still want you, Slim, but I ain't puttin' up with that shit."

"I promise not to let it happen again. Forgive me?"

"Don't worry 'bout it. I accept your apology."

As I approached the house I called Linda and told her to come down. She was downstairs and walking toward me in less than 5 minutes.

"Slick, please don't mention what happened back there to my wife in law. I'm ashamed of myself," Slim said.

"It'll be our little secret," I assured Slim just before Linda got in the car.

****

During our ride to work I was in my own little world. *Is this really worth it?* I asked myself. *Is this the profession I want to be in for rest of my life? What have I become? What kind of a monster would do something like this for money? What will be my fate if I continued to travel this road?* As the years went by my good conscience got stronger, making it harder for me to pimp. I thought of the family life I was missing, the normalcy. For the first time while in the game I was envious of squares. I wanted to go to work 8 hours per day and live a simple life.

Cash showed me the nice side of the game: the glamor, the pretty women, and the money. But he never showed me the dark side. He never told me that I would have to stoop so low to make it work. He never told me that I would be dealing with junkies, rapist, venereal diseases, and mentally unstable women. Although I put on a front as if everything was OK, I didn't like what I was doing. I couldn't stand myself. I didn't feel comfortable in my own skin. I knew that I had to do something else with my life; I knew I had to get out of the game.

Suddenly, I heard sirens. I peeked in the rear view mirror.

"Daddy, it's the police," Linda said in a panic.

I knew the routine. I pulled over, put my hands on the steering wheel, and told the girls to stay calm.

The cop walked up to the car. "License, registration, and insurance card," he demanded as he shined his flashlight in the car. I gave him what he asked for. He walked back to his cruiser and stayed there for about 20 minutes. Another cop car showed up. Things weren't looking good.

"Would you mind if I search the car?" the new officer asked.

I gave him permission. The girls and I got out and stood on the sidewalk until the officer was done searching. When he was done he walked back over to us with a small plastic baggie with what looked like crack cocaine in it and a glass stem used for smoking the powerful drug.

"Who does this belong to?" he asked.

I looked at Slim. She looked at the ground while nervously picking her right forefinger nail with her left thumb. Perhaps she didn't hear the cop.

None of us answered. He asked a second time, but still no one spoke up to claim it.

Once it became apparent that Slim didn't mind letting someone else take the rap for her drugs I tilted my head to the left and stared at her with vengeful, piercing red eyes in disbelief. My nostrils flared and I bit my bottom lip as I fought the urge to yell "Speak up, you know it's yours!" I looked back at the officer, took a deep breath, and prepared myself for his next move. He looked directly at me, raised his eyebrows, and happily smiled before his cold words hit me.

"Mr. Smalls, we are going to have to take you down and book you for criminal possession of a controlled substance," the cop told me. "Since it is your car you're in possession of it."

I heard the other cop tell the girls, "You girls can go, but we're impounding the car, so you should get all of your belongings."

"What am I gonna do?" Linda yelled, then walked to the back of the car, sat on the curb, and cried. I heard her sniffling. Slim walked off. I never saw her again.

I don't know anything about that officer. I tried pleading my case.

"You can tell it to the judge in the morning, but for now, turn around and put your hands behind your back," the cop said as he grabbed my arm and physically forced me to turn around.

****

The police took me to the 77th Percent, where I spent the night in the holding pen. The holding pen was disgusting, with trash all over the cells, derelicts lying on the floor, and the reek of bodily waste from the stopped-up toilet 9 of us shared. At 6am an officer came to the cell and passed me breakfast through the cell bars. I had a box of cereal and a container of milk.

The good thing about being locked up in New York was that I got to see a judge within 24 hours. Other states can hold a prisoner for months before bringing him before a judge.

"Listen up for your name. When you hear it step out!" an officer yelled.

Everyone whose name was called stepped out and lined up outside of the cell gate. The officer handcuffed us together with one long chain with handcuffs attached to it. We were led to a huge truck that had seats in the back. Everyone took a seat, and we were transported to the Brooklyn Criminal Court on Schermerhorn Street in downtown Brooklyn.

I sat in the holding pen of the courthouse for at least three hours until an officer began calling names again. I was called to go into a little room that was attached to the cell. The room had a metal stool in it that was fixed to the floor and a four-by-four hole in the wall with metal bars in the middle that separated me from freedom. A public defender stood on the other side of the bars with documents describing my case and what I was accused of. It was obvious by the tone in the public defender's voice and the look on his face that he didn't care whether I was guilty or not. I was just another file in his case load. He told me that if I pled guilty the prosecutor would agree to give me only one-and-a-half to three years in state prison, or I could take my case to trial and face a maximum of 7 years in the state penitentiary.

"What?" I asked, knowing I didn't hear him correctly.

"You're facing 7 years in the penitentiary," he repeated.

I gulped, then sat there frozen, just staring through the cell bars in his direction. My natural color left my face. I must have sat there staring for at least 30 seconds. When the initial shock began to wear off I wiped my brow. Although I felt a little lightheaded I tried to focus on the situation.

I opened my mouth and tried to speak but nothing came out. I rubbed my head and sighed. When I was finally able to speak I could hardly recognize my voice. It was raspy and lower than usual.

"What do you suggest I do?"

"Well, briefly tell me your side of the story."

"The police pulled me over and searched my car. One of my passengers stashed her drugs in my car but she didn't fess up to the crime so I was charged with possession," I managed to say with some clarity as I was getting my voice back.

"That's exactly what your transcript says, so the police weren't lying. Plead not guilty and I will ask the judge to consider releasing you on your own recognizance. That will give you time to think about it while free. If he doesn't agree to R.O.R, how much of a bail are you able to make today?"

"I don't have any money at all, sir. I'm unemployed." Telling the courts that I had money was a sure way to make them ask for some. Only an idiot would say they could afford a bail.

The Public Defender opened his briefcase and put my file in a stack of other files. He then pulled out another file. "I'll do the best I can to get you out of here today, Mr. Smalls. Can you call Kevin Smith in, please?" he asked while opening Kevin's file. That was my cue that my time was up.

****

"Ricky Smalls!" the guard yelled.

"Yes that's me," I answered and walked toward the exit gate.

The guard unlocked the cell gate and opened it for me to step out. Once I was on the outside of the cell the guard handcuffed me again. Then he walked me into the court room, where I sat patiently and waited for my case to be called.

"Number fifteen on the calendar, Ricky Smalls, step up!" the court officer yelled.

I walked up to the podium, stood next to the public defender, and faced the judge.

"Mr. Smalls, you're being charged with 220.21, Criminal Possession of a Controlled Substance in the first degree. How do you plead?"

"Not guilty," I answered.

The judge turned to the prosecutor, a tall pretty blonde in a tight brown skirt suit that captured every one of her sexy curves. "How do you want to proceed, Ms. Whitiker?" the judge asked.

Ms. Whitiker began trying to make me look like a bad guy. "Your Honor, this isn't the first time Mr. Smalls has been in trouble with the law. My records indicate that he was arrested in 1985 for sale and possession of marijuana for which he received five years' probation. Mr. Smalls obviously hasn't learned his lesson, so I'm recommending that we set his bail in the amount of two hundred thousand dollars."

Suddenly the prosecutor didn't look sexy to me anymore.

The judge looked at the public defender. "Counselor," he said, letting the public defender know that it was his turn to speak on my behalf.

"Your Honor, Mr. Smalls hasn't been in trouble with the law in 12 years. His address has been verified, so I'm recommending you release Mr. Smalls on his own recognizance."

There was a short silence as the judge read something. Then, for the first time, the judge looked me square in the eye and said, "Bail set at $50,000, cash or bond."

The officer that was standing behind me grabbed me by the arm and led me back to the holding pen.

Usually when I got into nasty situations like incarceration my family were the first people that I called. I felt bad; I was embarrassed, but what was I to do? I called my brother Pete, gave him the combination to my safe, and he came and got me before the Rikers Island bus got to the courthouse to take me to our city jail.

168

"I told you to leave them hoes alone. I'm not coming to get your ass no more!" Pete yelled as soon as he saw me.

Talk about mad. I could have fried an egg on his head.

Nothing was more uncomfortable than my ride home in the hot seat. Mortification surrounded me. I couldn't look Pete in the eye. My cheeks were so hot they could have caught fire. I stared at my feet, hoping he wouldn't notice how embarrassed I was. I wished the ground would open up and swallow me.

Chapter 16

It was 1997, and Rudolph Giuliani was the mayor of New York City. Under the Giuliani administration anyone convicted of two felonies had to go to prison; it was mandatory. For the following nine months my case was adjourned and rescheduled, which bought me more free time. Eventually I knew I would have to go to prison because I decided to plead guilty. According to the Public Defender a jury would probably convict me because of my prior felony conviction and because possession is ¾ of the law. He explained that the odds of me winning at trial were slim.

By the time I plead guilty my offer went up to two to four years. Usually the offer goes up when the prosecutor knows they have a solid case against the defendant. I did my bid in The Willard Program, a military boot camp-style prison for drug offenders. For the next five months my name was 97R5301.

I instructed Linda to work on a small track in Bay Ridge, Brooklyn, while I was away. I felt it was safer because pimps very rarely worked there women there so she didn't have to worry about them harassing her.

Before getting to my home prison I had to go through the whole lock-up process from the beginning. Again it was the nasty bull pen therapy. I must have stayed in there for two days, sleeping on floors and hard benches. The guards kept the air conditioning up high to keep the germs down, but they didn't give me a blanket. While in the bull pen I psyched myself up for my trip to Rikers Island. Rikers was a very dangerous city jail. Many of my friends had come back from Rikers with horror stories of how they had to hurt someone or someone hurt them for something as minute as a cookie. I thanked God for putting people like Jose and Cool in my life. If it wasn't for them and a few others in my neighborhood I wouldn't have lasted a day on Rikers Island. If anyone had approached me in a negative or aggressive way my mind was set to kill— not to win but to kill.

As soon as I got to intake I made a shank and kept it in my underwear between the elastic and my skin. When the guards weren't looking I sharpened it on the cement between the bricks of the cell walls. I never smiled, and I never made friends. I never showed any signs of weakness.

The telephone was a big deal on Rikers Island. Just before I got there some kid got stabbed in the head fourteen times for using the phone. Inmates always fought over the phone, so every house I lived in I made sure the phone was the first place I went. I picked it up and made a call even if I didn't need to. It was my way of establishing my position in the house. I figured if there was going to be a problem I might as well get it out of the way in the beginning because I had to live there, and I was determined to be comfortable in my home.

I spent two weeks on Rikers, two weeks in Ulster State Correctional Facility, and four months in Willard. Willard and Ulster were state-run prisons. I had a little more freedom in the prisons than in the city jail. The inmates seemed to be more relaxed in the prisons, probably because our sentences were final.

At 5:30 every morning a military-style horn sounded over the loud speaker. I had twenty minutes to use the bathroom and stand in formation for roll call. After every inmate was counted I had another twenty minutes to make my bed, get dressed in my gray sweat suit, and be back in formation to go to the black top. We were all led to the black top every morning for exercise. The black top was a huge pavement made of black asphalt. I marched, jogged, did pushups, stood in formation, and sung cadence on the black top.

After four months of Willard I was released to intensive parole supervision at 110 Dekalb Avenue in Brooklyn New York. My parole officer was very strict in the beginning. I did everything I could to get her to lighten up and because I really wanted to make some changes in my life.

****

My brother Pete got me a job as a Network Administrator contractor. The jobs were contracts given to small companies when Verizon and other national companies had too big of a work load. I loved the work I was doing. Just knowing that I was the cause of fixing someone's telephone or computer was so satisfying. Ever since I was a kid tinkering with old televisions I had a passion for fixing things, preferably computers or some sort of network equipment. Pete and I worked side by side, and he taught me on the job. I learned to dress cables, route them, test, and terminate them. I learned to build racks to lay the cables on. I swapped Verizon's old telecommunications equipment for new equipment. I was very inquisitive. I asked a lot of questions. Some of the questions my brother didn't have answers to so I did my own research.

I kept Linda around to make sure I made ends meet when there were gaps in my contracting projects and because she had no place else to go. The jobs that I was getting only lasted for a few months before I'd be unemployed but I knew I would eventually find a permanent job so I could leave the street life for good.

I went on as many job interviews as I could, but the same dreaded question kept coming up: "Have you ever been convicted of a felony?" I asked my parole officer how to answer that question and she said to "always tell the truth." I did, but every door I tried said "NO FELONS ALLOWED."

I became frustrated from all of the rejections and eventually started sliding back into the game. I was hurting inside, but I wore my happy mask because telling anyone in the game that I was about to lose my mind was not good for business. Most of the time the only people that I had around me were hoes, and they were expecting me to keep them from losing *their* minds. I became very introverted and anti sociable. I held in every bad thing that I'd witnessed in the game that had made me uncomfortable for nearly 20 years. I was like a balloon filled to the max with bad air. I was ready to explode. There were a few times when I had to let it out on Pete and a few other close family members.

As my life changed, family events became a thing of the past. The music that I listened to changed to more depressing music, music that described what I was going through. I started arguments with the girls just because I was miserable. I hated my life. I'd gotten to the point of hoping someone would kill me because wherever people went when they died had to be a much better then where I was.

Chapter 17

"Rise and shine!" I yelled.

"Mornin' Daddy," Linda said, her voice cracking.

"Here's a buck fifty; go buy you a new outfit." I pulled out my huge bank roll and peeled off a crisp one hundred dollar bill and a fifty. I left the money on the night stand and exited the room.

I took a hot shower and got dressed in the new green leisure suit I had bought the day before from the Kings Plaza Mall. I went outside and felt the cool, fresh breeze pass through my leisure suit; it felt good. I got in my car and put on some old-school music by Curtis Mayfield: "Superfly." Once again I was in hot pursuit of a prostitute.

I went to Queens Plaza. Most prostitutes under a pimp's instructions would have been in at that time of

178

the evening unless they didn't make their quota the night before. In that case they would be mad, tired, and their feet would be hurting. I used to call it the mad hour.

After riding around the track for about 30 minutes I ran into a little black girl wearing black Pum Pum shorts with the top to match. I almost missed her because she was hiding in the cut to block herself from the wind. I pulled up to the curb and said, "Hop in." She did. I had seen her a few times before, walking with a tall skinny Spanish junkie.

"Wanna hang out with me for a little while?" I asked after driving around the block.

"No thanks, I'm workin'. Do you want some fun?" she answered.

"Baby Doll, I know you're working, and I commend you on being so brave, hiding in the cut until you see a trick because the police are pickin' up, smart move," I replied, skillfully dodging her question.

"The police are picking up? I didn't know that." She sounded surprised.

"You didn't see the van go by full of hoes just before I picked you up?"

"They did?"

"Yeah. Good thing I came around and saved you." I began driving toward the bridge. "So you wanna hang out with me this morning or what??

"OK but just for a little while, until it cools off," she replied as she took her feet out of her cheap, run-down shoes.

"Cool."

I drove down 21st Street and ran my mouth in an attempt to distract her long enough to get her away from the neighborhood without her noticing. I was headed toward home by way of Manhattan.

The phone rang three times. I didn't want to answer it because I thought it might be Linda on the other end and she might say something loud enough to be heard through the receiver and reveal my plans for my new prospect. Finally I answered while turning the receiver down at the same time.

"What up, Slick? How the day treatin' you?" came from the receiver. It was Mo.

"What da deal, Mo Money?" I responded.

"Been tryin' to get a hold of Cash and tell him lay low 'cause of that shit that went down this morning."

"What shit?"

"Cash shot an imam, he ain't tell you?"

"Naw, I haven't spoken to him today."

"I don't wanna go into detail over the phone, but holla at your bro."

"OK, I'll do that, I'm a little busy right now Mo.

I'll hit you later."

"Cool, handle your business," he said just

before hanging up.

"What's your name, Baby Girl?" I asked after

Mo hung up.

"Crystal."

"Listen Crystal, it's obvious your feet are

hurting because you need a pair of shoes. Those are

Payless shoes; they cost under $10. Your hair is a mess

and your nail polish is chipped. How do you expect to

be at your full potential in that condition? How do

expect a trick with good money to want to date you?

You gotta look like money to make money."

Crystal took offense. I had started out wrong; I

should have started easy.

"Why you tryin' to dis? You don't even know me," Crystal said. I could see she was getting angry. I was about to blow it.

I stayed in control of the conversation, attempting to fix it. "Crystal, I apologize. I was wrong for comin' down on your appearance." I decided to take a different approach. "I know you probably don't recognize me, but I've seen you around here. I know your man, Donald. I've known him for a while. He's on drugs, so it's like you're just doing this for nothing. I know he's just wastin' all your money on drugs. If you're going to struggle like this I suggest you get a job. Squares struggle; pimps and hoes live like royalty."

We used to call Crystal's man Donald the Doorman because he would stand in front of the diner opening doors for anyone that wanted to enter or exit and then ask them for change. He wore the same khaki suit every day and he was way overdue for a shave.

"I know I'm a mess, and you're right, but I don't know what to do. I can't get a job; I didn't finish high school. I can't go back to my parents' house because my mom kicked me out when she found out I'm pregnant," Crystal said as she broke down crying.

I braced myself and collected my words before I spoke. "Don't worry, Baby Girl, everything is going to be alright. God has a plan for you. You are God's creation, and you were put on the earth to have a purpose in life. I know your days look dark now, but the Lord will never put anything before you that's too hard for you to handle. With me on your side I promise you'll be OK."

She looked up at me with watery eyes and asked, "With you on my side? What are you talking about?"

"I'll help you if you'll allow me to. I will do the best I can to help, but there are some things I need to tell you before we go any further."

"What?" she asked, looking at me as if she was expecting the worst.

"Baby Girl, I'm in the same profession as you are. That's what I was doing out there."

"Are you a pimp?" she asked as if she was scared.

"I am."

"Why you didn't tell me you were pimpin'?!" she yelled.

"You didn't ask," I replied.

"I gotta get out of this car. I'm not even 'posed to be talking to you," Crystal said angrily.

"Be easy, Baby Girl. I'm not a kidnapper, I'm a pimp. If you wanna get out here you can, or I can just drive you back to where I picked you up, like a gentlemen should."

The phone rang right on cue. I excused myself and answered it, not caring who was on the other end now that the cat was out of the bag.

"Daddy, I just found this nice outfit I'ma wear tonight," came from the receiver.

"Just a minute. I'm in traffic, and don't need another ticket," I replied as I put the phone on speaker. "So what you do with the $150 I gave you this mornin'?"

Linda's voice came through the receiver loud and clear. "I bought a black strapless spandex dress, a pair of 7 inch red stiletto heels, a bra, and a pair of thongs."

"Oh, you gonna be a track star tonight, huh?"

"Yep, and I'm getting my hair done. I'm at the beauty salon now."

"What time are you going to be done?"

"Probably around four. Can we go out early tonight?"

"Sounds like a plan to me."

"What you doin', Daddy?"

"I'm just out pimpin'."

"Catch any new hoes?"

"I'm working on it."

"Ooh Daddy, the beautician is calling me, I gotta go."

Linda hung up. I could tell Crystal was interested in my conversation with Linda because she immediately asked, "How many hoes you got?"

"Two including you," I answered.

She showed me her pearly white teeth. It was the first time I saw her smile since she'd been in the car.

"You down, or do you want me to take you back to your crackhead man?" I had to drop a little salt on him while asking.

"I don't know…"

"What have you got to lose? You ain't got nothin'," I said, hoping I wasn't being too hard on her.

"I guess I'll give it a try," Crystal answered.

We spoke for a very long time. Crystal had a broad vocabulary. She seemed to be very well-rounded despite not finishing high school. Crystal said she loved to read and that explained her vocabulary. She was an interesting girl and extremely pretty. Her intellect turned me on more than her beauty. We spoke for hours about so many things we lost track of time. Crystal was also raised in the Kingdom Hall; her mom was a Jehovah's Witness. After about an hour of speaking to her I didn't want her on my team. I wanted her to do bigger and better things with her life.

"Crystal... There's other avenues that you can take. You don't have to do what you are doing." I couldn't believe what I was saying.

"What do you suggest I do? I'm homeless. The only clothing I have is what's on my back and two other outfits on top of the roof of a factory building in Queens. The only reason why I was with Donald is for protection. I have no one on my side. I don't have any brothers or sisters. I have an extended family in Georgia but I don't even know them. I can't and won't go back home to my mother because my mom is so blinded by my abusive stepfather that she won't even believe me when I tell her he's been hurting me and that her soon-to-be grandson will also be her stepson. With no job and no education, what else can I do?"

Crystal's story was touching me in a way that I didn't want to be touched. She was getting to my heart. *Damn that good conscience! Why can't it just stay put?*

As the years went by it became harder to keep my emotions in check. Some of the hardship stories I heard broke down my invisible, protective wall and gave the girls a glimpse of the real Rick. I put my head down because I didn't want her to see the hurt I was feeling for her. Parents were practically giving their children to pimps. I've spoken to several girls with similar situations: parents beat or raped them, and the government doesn't give a damn about them. It's messed up, but sometimes a pimp is their only option. A pimp really can be their savior.

"You never give up," I told her. "Keep your head up and believe you will be OK. You gotta believe in yourself. You have to be strong if you are going to make it out here." I was also speaking to myself because I had given myself the same advice.

Crystal continued, "The pressure I feel every day is sometimes too much for me. Sometimes I cry all night. I'm pregnant for Christ's sake; is this how I have to live? Is this how I have to raise my child?"

Crystal broke down sobbing. I embraced her. I gave her a genuine hug, and I really felt for her.

"You don't have to run game on me," Crystal said through her tears. "You don't have to even care about me. Right now all I need is a decent roof over my head and a little time to think. I'll pay you. I'm only in it temporarily though, so get what you can. When it's over let's part in peace."

"Crystal, there is other ways to make money. Why don't you try the Walter Hoving Home? They come around the tracks trying to save hoes all the time."

"They approached me a few times, but I don't need anyone forcing their religion on me."

"Welfare is always an option," I tried again. I was fishing for the right words to say to get her out of the game, but she was right. She really didn't have many options.

"I applied for welfare last month, but by the time they give me anything I'll starve to death. It sounds like you don't want me; am I missing something? No pimp is going to suggest I do anything but work for him," Crystal said.

"Well Crys…" I began.

"It's Crystal," she corrected me.

"Excuse me, Crystal. We are sort of in similar situations. I don't wanna be in this life anymore either. It's hurting me mentally. It's breaking me down more and more every day. Women are going to jail for doing things that I instructed them to do. They are putting themselves in danger every night. I don't like what I am doing. I don't have any friends. I am always lonely because I can't trust anyone. I can't get a job because of my record. I have a record because of the path I chose. I paid my debt but I am still being punished. If I can't get a job what else am I to do? So I identify with what you're saying, and I feel your pain. I sincerely want to help you, not hurt you. You and I have been hurt enough." I realized I was dumping my frustrations on her.

"We have to play with the cards we were dealt until we are dealt a better hand," Crystal said. It made sense.

I really wanted Crystal in a different way. She was definitely girlfriend material. I wish I had met her under different circumstances.

I called Linda back to let her know she had a new wife in law.

"Daddy, can you pick me up from the beauty salon?" Linda asked.

"OK, I'll be there in 20 minutes. But we got company, so be outside," I replied before hanging up.

When I pulled up in front of the salon I could see the look of rage in Linda's face as she walked to the car. She just stood in front of the driver's side window for a few seconds before asking, "Can I sit in my seat?"

I told Crystal to hop in the back. She hopped over the seat with no problem, showing her pretty brown ass cheeks as her ass went up in the air, and the rest of her young sexy body followed.

When Linda got in I immediately set the tone. "Damn girl, your hair looks nice! They really whipped your wig huh?"

Linda smiled. I touched her smooth silky brown hair, smelled it, and caressed it with the back of my hand. I made like I was really interested. I kissed her on the forehead.

"Wow, you are so sexy," I said. It was true; Linda was a very sexy girl. All of a sudden Linda was in a good mood and forgot all about her new wife in

194

law. "Where are your manners?" I asked with a surprised look on my face.

"What? Ohh I'm sorry, Daddy." Linda turned around and introduced herself to Crystal. "Daddy she's cute." Linda looked at Crystal as if Crystal was a steak and she hadn't eaten in weeks.

"If you behave yourself I'll let you have her first," I replied.

Linda smiled uncontrollably. I looked in the mirror and Crystal was smiling too. It was a love connection, a match made in heaven.

We drove back to the house to get a little rest and get ready for the night. I slept in the living room because it seemed like the two of them were hitting it off well. After about a half hour I was awaken by loud love-making noises coming from the bedroom, but I quickly fell back to sleep.

Chapter 18

Both girls were dressed and ready for work by 10pm. Linda loaned Crystal a tight-fitting blue dress and a pair of six inch black pumps. The girls looked great.

I took them to Queens Plaza because the Manhattan track was hot with police. Cashmere had created an issue with the Muslims. There were already a few familiar faces in Queens Plaza when I got there. The first one I ran into was Mo Money. He was standing on the corner talking to some guy I hadn't met. Mo introduced me to him.

"Remember dark-skinned Billy with the Chinese bitch? He drove a black Cadillac?"

"Yeah I member Bill, Dollar Bill," I answered.

"This is his brother Slimy."

I shook Slimy's hand and introduced myself.

"Slick Rick."

Slimy was a tall, medium-built brown-skinned man. He wore his hair short and slicked back. There was a diamond stud earring in his right ear and one diamond ring on each pinky, one yellow and the other blue. The yellow diamond ring on the left hand was in the shape of a crown. His black and white pinstriped Armani Exchange two-piece suit with matching tie and handkerchief complimented his black and white alligator shoes made by Mauri. Slimy's nails were well-manicured and I could smell the expensive cologne he wore as he came close enough to shake my hand. I could tell by his soft skin that the man never worked a day in his life. His hands were as soft as a baby's ass.

Linda was doing well, but Crystal was missing in action for the entire night. I was unhappy. I knew that at the end of the night I would have a pocket full of cash but I would still be unhappy. I did not want to be doing what I was doing to make a living.

Later that morning Linda walked over to me smiling. "Can I go to the diner and get some breakfast before we go home?" she asked.

"Go. I'll pick you up in 20 minutes," I quickly answered. I wanted to get her away from me as fast as possible because my mind was preoccupied with so many other things.

I stuck around for about 20 more minutes to wait for Crystal. Finally I headed for the diner to pick Linda up.

After noticing that we were headed home without her wife in law Linda asked, "Where's Crystal?"

"I don't know where she's at, but it's about to be square hour. Let's get out of here. She got my number." "Square hour" was the hours when the squares were in the streets. Those were also the hours we slept.

I worried about Crystal that entire day. I kept my phone next to my head while I slept and hoped she would call. Crazy thoughts went through my head of all the things that could have happened to her. I couldn't figure out what made Crystal much different than the others. Why did I care about her so much?

Chapter 19

I kept the volume of the music up during our ride to work to let Linda know I didn't feel like talking. I was in my own little world. I thought about Crystal and where she could be. I wondered if she went back to her man or chose another pimp. I thought of the apartment I would get for Crystal and the baby. I thought of things we both could do to change the direction of our lives and live happily ever after. I was worried about Crystal, but I didn't want Linda to know just how much I cared about her because I knew Linda would become jealous. Even though she wasn't into me I knew it would cause a problem.

When I got to the track the first person I ran into was Slime, riding with a dude named Prince. Prince was a light-skinned guy with an old school Afro. He wore a leather biker jacket, and I could tell him and

Slime were real good friends by the way they carried on. I hopped in and rode around with them for a while. We took a ride up 8th Avenue in Manhattan. There I was introduced to Preacher. Preacher was a former player who found his escape from the streets in the Bible. He would always preach the Word of God to us from what he called the Good Book. Every player in the area respected Preach.

Slimy pulled over so Preacher could get in.

"Hey Preach, how they treatin' you?" Prince turned around to shake Preacher's hand.

Slimy said, "Preach, this is a good buddy of mine. His name is Slick, and he lives up to his name. He's 'Shmere's younger brother."

Cashmere used to hate that name.

"Pleased to meet you," Preach said as he extended his hand for me to shake it.

Preach and I hit it off well from the beginning. He was a very interesting man. I admired how he went through all the bullshit the streets had to offer and ended up on top, meaning he was happy, content, and out of the life. I also admired how he mentored players and showed them how there were other ways to be successful. Preach was a good guy, and I knew that we would become friends. Preach rode around with us for about a half hour before we dropped him off at the bus terminal on 42nd Street and 8th Ave.

I had to ask Slime, "How did you get the name Slimy?"

He chuckled and told me the story behind the name. "Before I got knocked off I had a handicapped bitch. She had cerebral palsy; I would prop her up on a pole on the corner, and the tricks loved her. Man, Slick, the bitch paid me like a slot machine, but she couldn't pronounce my name. My real name is Sammy but she unintentionally called me Slimy. Man, cats would die laughing when they heard the bitch call me. Then the name just stuck with me."

I laughed so hard tears came to my eyes. He really was a slimy motherfucker to pimp a retarded woman.

Slime dropped me off on the track at about 4am. I saw both Crystal and Linda standing about a block apart. I got in the car and tapped the horn. Both of them began walking to the car.

"Where you been?" I asked Crystal as soon as she entered.

"My stupid Craigslist trick picked me up and took me to his house in Long Island. He gets so paranoid every time I used the phone. He thought I was trying to set him up. I'm sorry I couldn't call you."

Crystal handed me $1100, but I was just glad she was home. I really missed her. I kept trying to control myself and stay within the games boundaries.

Falling in love with a ho was way out of bounds. But I

couldn't help it; I'd smile every time I saw her. When

she was close to me I couldn't keep from caressing her

pretty brown skin. It always felt good being around her.

I didn't even think about money when Crystal was

around.

I took her out to breakfast. While we ate she

encouraged me not to give up looking for a job. She

said to turn over every stone and eventually someone

would hire me. I really appreciated the encouragement.

Chapter 20

During the day I searched the internet for jobs. I searched Monster.com, Craigslist.org and Careerbuilder.com. I built a resume using a copy of my brother's for an outline. There were large gaps in my work history, but I filled them in by changing the dates on the very few temporary contract jobs that I had managed to get. I also filled in the gaps with companies that went out of business. I had friends who owned their own businesses who agreed to say I worked for them for a number of years if any one called them for a reference. I made it a point to send at least ten resumes per week to potential employers, and soon companies were getting back to me to set up interviews. I must have gone on at least two interviews per month.

****

"Charles Moore of Verizon. May I speak to Mr. Ricky Smalls please?"

"Speaking. How may I help you?" I asked as I yawned, awakening from a short nap.

"Mr. Smalls, we interviewed you approximately a month ago for the position of Field Technician. Do you recall?"

"Yes I remember. How are you, Mr. Moore?"

"I'm fine, thank you. The reason I am calling is because I feel you would be a good candidate for the position. Are you still interested?"

"Yes I am," I replied excitedly.

"Good! Would you be available to come down for orientation next week?"

"Sure," I replied, fully awake and with a big smile on my face.

"We're meeting in the cafeteria of the same building you were interviewed in at 9am Monday morning. Can you make it?"

"Yes, I'll be there 9 o'clock sharp!" I said, still very excited.

"Just show security your identification and he will direct you to the cafeteria. Dress down, because all you will be doing on Monday is filling out some administrative paperwork and looking at a short film to give you an overview of the company and what is expected of our Field Technicians. I look forward to working with you. See you on Monday."

I replied, "Thank you very much, Mr. Moore. Enjoy your day."

I experienced an incredible feeling of relief. Finally, my prayers were answered. I got on my knees and thanked God for answering my prayers. Praying was something that I did regularly. After praying I called Crystal to tell her the good news.

I knew that employment with Verizon meant I would have a good long-term career with benefits. I'd be able to take care of Crystal, the baby, and myself without breaking the law. I walked around with a grin for the rest of the week.

****

When I got to Verizon for the orientation on Monday morning there were five other people there to fill out the final paperwork and watch the film. I filled out my W2 form, read and signed the employee agreement, and a Verizon secretary made copies of my driver's license and Social Security card. I watched the short film and was out of there within an hour. I was given some paperwork to be filled out by a physician and was told that a Verizon representative would call me to let me know when my training would begin.

Verizon made an appointment for me to go to a clinic in my area. It was in walking distance from my house. I took the physical with confidence. I felt like I was in pretty good shape, but I did have a little doubt. One time Pete blew a good job because a physical revealed that he had a heart condition.

I got a phone call from a Verizon representative the following Monday. "Good evening. May I speak to Mr. Smalls please?"

"Mr. Smalls speaking."

"This is Clara Sierra of Verizon, I'm just calling to let you know that you passed the physical and your training starts on the 1st of November, a week from today."

"Thank you; I'll mark that day on my calendar."

"Have a great day. We look forward to working with you."

"You do the same, Ms. Sierra. Goodbye."

For the first time in my life I was proud of myself. I felt like I was a part of society, like they had finally let me back in. When people asked me what I did for a living I wouldn't have to hesitate while thinking of a quick lie. I could simply answer "I'm a Field Technician for Verizon." How cool is that?

Chapter 21

Slimy drove through the track in Queens in his three year old Jaguar Vanden Plas. I thought, *Slimy is really doing well in the business.* Mo and I stared in admiration as Slimy pulled over in front of us, got out, and immediately started bragging.

"I see you done came up, Slime!" Mo yelled.

Slimy loved to showboat. "Man, that old white bitch I got just robbed the trick for $40,000. Lame went to sleep and left the safe open. Next morning I was helping the Jaguar dealer open up." He laughed as he puffed his chest out. "I knocked that pretty motherfucker and had a few grand left." He pointed to his car.

Slimy always spoke loud enough for everyone to hear him. As he stood there popping the collar on the maroon suit he probably only bought to match the color of his car, the track seemed to come alive.

Slimy drove back and forth though the track making passes at Linda that night. It took me by surprise; I couldn't believe he was doing that to me. I thought we were friends. I made the mistake of trusting a snake. Slimy knew some things about Linda and Crystal that he shouldn't have. He began using some of the things I told him to try to get into Linda's head and con her. He would ride by and shout to her, "Slick was talkin' 'bout sendin' you back to the shelter. He said you too possessive and it's causing problems!" He was trying to find the right combination of words to get her upset enough to leave me and possibly work for him. We all did that. It was legal in the game, but we didn't do it to people we were tight with. I thought Slimy and I were tight, but I was obviously wrong.

"You need to come on and get with me before you end up homeless. I only got room for one more, so you better hurry up!" Slimy yelled.

It would have worked out perfectly if Linda had gone with Slimy since the game was over for me and I was retiring Crystal. I figured I'd take care of her until the baby was old enough to go to some sort of day care. Then Crystal could get a job. I was still upset by the way he was crossing me though. How could he betray me so blatantly? The fucking bastard.

I knew that Slimy's betrayal was my fault. I shouldn't have trusted him. I had let my guard down. Cash told me early on that I had no friends in the game. He said, "If you want friends you're in the wrong game. This is a cold and lonely game." That night I felt it.

Slime drove down 38th Street several times that night, which was the block Linda liked to work on. He parked his car in front of Linda; Linda took off walking down the street. Slimy got out of his car and slowly walked behind Linda, making passes as he walked. I don't know what Slime said to her, but it looked like he had her attention. Linda stopped walking, turned around, and stared at him. She stood there for a while as if she was interested in what he had to say. Then he walked back to his car and drove off down the street toward Queens Boulevard.

Other pimps saw what was going on. Mo gave me some advice: "Jug at his hoes the same way he's doing you." Blue said, "You gotta stop that fool; he couldn't do that to me."

Chapter 22

.

"Slick, Linda is too possessive. It's annoying. I'm not a lesbian; I just want to have fun. I wanna be with you, but it seems like the only time we can be alone is when she's on a date. When I kissed you on your cheek the other night she got upset. Can you talk to her?" Crystal asked as she sat on the couch next to me.

"You've been here over a month now. Why are you just telling me this?"

I should have known that their sleeping together would cause problems. I felt I was slipping. I should have known how Crystal felt before she even told me.

Crystal continued, "I didn't wanna cause any problems. I want to be with you—you my dude—but I don't think Linda will understand."

That night I explained to Linda that Crystal needed her own place because she was getting ready for motherhood. Linda said she understood but I could tell by the look on her face that she really didn't.

A few days later I found an apartment for Crystal. It was my plan to find her one even before we had the conversation about Linda because I wanted to be closer to her too.

****

Crystal and I were living like a happy couple most of the day. We were going through some sort of transformation to the square life, I enjoyed it. Crystal cooked breakfast in the morning and dinner was normally ready between 6 and 7 pm. It was hard for me to keep a schedule and be home in time for my meals because of the streets and other women that I had in my life, but I tried, and most of the time I succeeded.

Two months had gone by, and Crystal's belly was growing fast. I knew she loved her unborn child. I let her know just how much I loved the child too and how much of a good, loving father I would be to the child when it arrived. She was happy to hear that I wanted the baby just as bad as she did. I knew the baby was going to do both of us some good. I knew it was going to bring us closer. I used to rub Crystal's belly and sing to my daughter. I wanted a girl.

Crystal's money was slowing down but I was OK with it; she was eating and sleeping a lot. She was bitching more and more but I dealt with it because I knew it was just the pregnancy that was causing her be annoying. I felt the streets were way too much stress for a pregnant woman, so I recommended that Crystal stay in the house and just take a few dates from her phone. Besides, I'd come to the point of not wanting another man touching her.

"Oh, I almost forgot, Slick: I got a date with my Craigslist trick. He's gonna pick me up in the city tonight," Crystal said one day.

I thought, *Damm, I don't want her to go. What can I do? I have to do something!* Being in the profession, it was crazy for me to even think like that. I tried to check myself.

"What's the matter, Slick?" Crystal asked.

I pulled her closer to me, put my arm around her, and kissed her on the lips.

"I don't want you to go," I said while trying extremely hard to control my emotions.

"What?" Crystal looked confused.

I was confused too. I didn't know what the hell was happening to me.

"I just know we can do other things, better things. I want you all to myself. There, I said it."

It was so hard for me to tell her how I felt because a pimp is not supposed to have those types of feelings for his women.

"Baby, we've had this conversation before. We have to do this 'til we can do better. The only other income you have is Linda, and I'm not gonna let another woman pull my weight."

That evening I dropped Crystal off on the corner of 24th Street and Broadway so she could meet her trick.

****

We worked in midtown Manhattan that night because the sailors were in town and they always spent a lot of money. Cash was on 11th Avenue when I got there, despite his beef with the Muslims. He was hollering at hoes, trying to recruit them. That was the norm for a pimp on 11th Ave. There was one pretty fat ass girl Cash just kept chasing. She was responding to what he said. I saw her smiling. I told Cash that her

219

man was a real fool and he should consider backing off of her. I knew Cash wasn't afraid of anyone out there but I just wanted to save him from problems.

About 15 minutes into his chasing that big beautiful fat ass girl up and down 11th Avenue, giving her what's come to be known as the Memphis Sweat, her man showed up. He was driving a white Monte Carlo with custom rims and a suped-up engine. He pulled right up on Cash and said something to him. He got out of his car and walked over to Cash. Cash just ignored him; I didn't understand why Cash wasn't preparing himself for defense considering what I had told him. I knew something was about to go down, because the man, Charles, was known for bullying pimps. I hurried towards them. When Charles got close to Cash, Cash just turned around and sucker punched him. Charles fell, and Cash jumped on top of him, hitting him repeatedly until someone ran over to them and pulled Cash off of him. Then Charles got off the ground, brushed himself off, and walked back to his car yelling at Cash. He opened the trunk and pulled out a gun. Cash took off running down the street when he saw the gun.

POP, POP, POP. I heard 3 shots. Good thing Cash had a head start. Cash ran toward10th Ave, jumped on the back of a moving UPS truck, and lived to fight another day.

I got a call from Cash about 10 minutes after the incident.

"You see that fool in the white Monte takin' shots at me? I beat the shit outa him! He had me running down the street like a bitch!"

Cash was frantic. I cut him off. "Calm down, Pimpin'. Where you at?"

"I'm on 28th and 8th."

"Get the hell out of here. The police is all over the place lookin' for both you and him."

He started again, "Man, I'ma kill that fool."

I cut him off again. "AT&T don't like that kind of talk, and I know you know better."

"I'll swing by your house tomorrow, we'll kick it." He hung up.

Cash made the track hot again. There was no sense staying out, so Linda and I went home early. Crystal hadn't called, and she didn't answer her phone all night. She always did that when she went with her Craigslist trick

****

First thing in the morning I went by Cash's house. As soon as I walked in the door I noticed his main girl Pleasure sitting on the couch talking to her wife in law, sporting two black eyes. I didn't ask any questions because it was none of my business, but the look on my face told her how I felt. Cash looked at her, then at me, and said very nonchalantly, "I found the bitch's stash spot. She had close to a $2500 stashed. Want some breakfast?"

I thought, *This motherfucker talked all that shit about not having to sleep with his hoes because he can give them eargasms all day, so why can't he find the right words to say to make Pleasure give up all the money?* I never understood pimps that hit their women. First off it was bad for business. Who would want to date a girl with two black eyes? They punch themselves in the wallet. I thought about the Christmas party at my grandmother's house on Lincoln Place in Brownsville, Brooklyn. I couldn't have been more than 5 years old. Dad was walking around my grandmother's house as if everything was OK while my mom sat in the living room sporting two black eyes. A feeling of rage overcame me. That was the first time I thought about

223

hurting my brother. Cashmere needed two black eyes of his own, and I was going to be the one to give them to him. When Cash turned around and walked back to the kitchen I saw the handle of his 9 millimeter in the small of his back.

"Naw, man, I'm cool, I just ate," I said, the thought of hurting Cash quickly leaving me.

"Just a minute," Cash mumbled. He looked at the women in the living room, just adjacent to the kitchen. "Get the fuck out of here!" he demanded. Both women immediately responded upon command. They got up and walked to the back with their heads down so as not to look at me. They weren't allowed to look at another pimp; doing so would've probably cost them an ass whipping.

Cash began telling me what happened the night before. He didn't know I saw the whole thing, but I thought I'd let him vent. After reliving the events of the night before Cash looked at me and said, "He's a dead man." I knew that Cash meant what he said. I sat and spoke to Cash for about another hour before I excused myself and went home.

Chapter 23

"Good afternoon Mr. Smalls, this is Mr. Moore of Verizon."

Yes Mr. Moore, how can I help you?" I smiled; I always became happy when a Verizon representative called me. Just the thought of speaking to someone at my new positive beginning made me happy. My training was set to start the following day.

"Mr. Smalls, we did a thorough check of everyone's applications, and it seems you didn't tell the truth when answering question number thirteen on the application, 'Have you ever been convicted of a felony?' Can you explain?"

He caught me off guard. I didn't have a good explanation. I tried desperately to find the right words. I had seconds to come up with something. Butterflies began flying around in my stomach. There was a sick feeling in pit of my belly and my heart raced. I squeezed the phone so hard my fingers went numb. I knew I was doomed if I didn't come up with a good reason for lying.

"Mr. Moore, that's over, and I paid my debt to society."

"I'm sorry, Mr. Smalls. I am going to have to terminate your employment at this time. It's company policy."

That's all it took. I'd lost my job before I even started. My hopes and dreams were just shattered by a phone call.

Once again the depression set in. I felt so worthless. The depression I felt was overwhelming. I started beating up on myself. What a loser I was. I was just a pimp, a dirty, lowdown, scum of the earth pimp. I hated my life and I hated myself. And where was Crystal? I needed the encouragement that she always gave, that pull up, that pat on the back that would help me get through another day

****

I took a ride to Midtown to find Preach; he always cheered me up. I found him on the corner of 43rd Street and 8th Avenue. We spoke for a long time, as we always did.

"Preach man, everybody runnin' 'round here talkin' 'bout how they sooo big pimpin' and parkin' they Caddies in the projects. Everybody frontin', Preach." I didn't feel like talking about what was really bothering me. I just needed someone to talk to.

"That's what the game is about, Slick. It's all a show. Nobody really has what they look like they have, and if they do you'd best believe their camp is filled with drugs. Them broads ain't doin' nothing but buyin' drug off these so-called pimps. What don't come out in the wash will come out in the rinse. How you think I

228

got knocked off? I'm guilty of the same thing. They caught me with six ounces of high-grade cocaine and five junkie broads. I did nearly 10 years behind that."

"Damn, Preach, this game don't love nobody."

"You ain't tellin' no lies, Slick. The faster you get out of it the better off you are gonna be."

"I'm working on it, Preach. I do have some plans on getting out of this mess."

Preach abruptly stopped walking to say something. I knew it was important by the way he looked me in the eyes.

"I took a liking to you when I first met you, Slick. I can tell you're an intelligent brother; you just got caught up in a crazy game. You remind me a lot of myself. When I was your age I saw the fancy cars, women, and money, and I was deceived. I asked a lot of questions because I had a strong quest for knowledge, but I was learning 'bout the wrong things. Things that were frowned upon in our society; things that could only bring me misery. I feel very strongly 'bout what I preach to you because I don't want you to make the same mistakes I've made."

I respected Preach. I knew he was speaking from the heart. I knew he cared.

He continued, "You see, Slick, no matter what you do in life you are going to have to pay." Preach opened his Bible, turned to Galatians 6:7-8, and read, "'Be not deceived; God is not mocked: for whatever a man soweth, that shall he also reap.'" Then he went on to explain. "You will reap bad and corrupt things when you do sinful things. You will reap everlasting life when you do good spiritual things. Something of an equal and opposite effect is going to come to you, and I hope you will be ready. What would you do if someone hurt or exploited your daughter? Don't answer that; I don't wanna be an accessory to murder."

We both laughed. I heard the ice cream truck in the middle of 47th Street between 8th and 9th Ave.

"Come on Preach," I said, "let me treat you to some ice cream."

When we approached the ice cream truck I ordered a chocolate comb and Preach had the same.

"See those kids over in that playground playing stick ball?" I asked the driver of the ice cream truck, pointing to the public school yard.

"Yeah, wassup?" said the driver.

"Make sure every one of those kids get some ice cream. Anything they want, my treat." I pulled out a crisp fifty dollar bill and handed it to the driver.

The driver pulled up to the playground, ringing his bell and screaming, "Free ice cream! Free ice cream!"

The kids stopped their game and came running towards the truck.

I always loved kids. It gave me a good feeling to put a smile on their faces. Just knowing that I made their day made me happy. Preach and I stood on the sidewalk behind the ice cream truck commenting on the happy faces.

"Look at that one," I said, pointing to a little fat white boy. I always thought the fat ones were cuter; they looked like teddy bears. He was smiling from ear to ear with chocolate ice cream all over his face. I laughed, then walked over and handed him a napkin.

"Hey Mister, you got change!" the driver yelled after all of the kids were served.

"Keep the change," I yelled back.

Preach and I walked to the bus terminal on 41st Street and 8th Avenue and talked for a couple more hours.

"Preach, I haven't heard from this one broad of mine in a couple a days. It's worrying me sick," I told him.

Preach said, "Just relax. Them girls run off all the time. I'm sure it will work itself out, so don't worry yourself. The Lord takes care of fools and babies."

I hated to speak to Preach about my business because he was so righteous, but I knew he had a lot of experience from his past and my troubles were really pressing me. Normally I would have called Cash, but I didn't want to hear his bullshit when he found out I had developed feelings for Crystal. Preach sensed I had feelings for Crystal right away.

"I have never seen you so concerned about a woman before," he said. "What makes this one so special? Let me find out: you've been shot by Cupid. You feelin' her, huh, Slick? Tell the truth and shame the devil."

233

"Yeah," I smiled. I got a warm fuzzy feeling inside when I thought about her. Crystal was my heart. "Man, Preach, we even talked about squaring up and getting married."

"Marriage!" Preach yelled, staring at me in disbelief.

"Yeah, marriage."

"Man, that's beautiful, but you know you and I are gonna have beef if I'm not the preacher that marries you."

I looked at Preach. "Well then we're just gonna have beef, because I found another preacher to marry us."

I could tell Preach was heartbroken when he heard that I wasn't using him. The look on his face told me just how hurt he was. He managed to say, "That's alright, Slick, congratulations anyway."

"Preach, you my best man!" I replied.

The biggest smile came across Preach's face. He gave me a hug.

"Thanks Slick. I'd be honored to be your best man."

"Hey Preach, I'm about to take it down," I said, because I was getting a little tired, and I'd got what I came for. As always, I felt much better after speaking to Preach. We shook hands and slapped each other on the back.

"Be careful," Preach said with sincerity.

On my way home I thought about some of the things Preach had said. Preach always gave me a positive message or something to think about.

Chapter 24

While driving through the Queens track I spotted Denise, Slimy's white girl, on the corner. She had blonde hair that fell to the middle of her back. She wore a pair of tight jeans that complimented her figure and a black short leather jacket. I didn't think she was attractive at all, but I wanted to give Slimy a taste of his own medicine. I didn't see Slimy's black girls. I drove around the block to give me time to think of the right thing to say. I pulled up on Denise and yelled, "What the hell you doin' out here in this weather while Slime is home fuckin' your wife in laws in a nice, warm house?! I guess he really don't like you! May be he don't like white girls; I think he's prejudiced! I guess you're out here working to support all three of them! You give a new meaning to the words 'white slavery'! You should come with me. I'll treat you way better than that!" I saw by the expression on her face that I'd got to her with what I said. She was listening. Even though she didn't come with me, at least I knew she would be going back home bitching about what I said. I was definitely causing trouble in Slime's house.

****

The following night we were all standing around on 21st Street talking pimp shit when Slimy said in a loud, obnoxious voice. "I see you givin' my bitch a lot of exercise out there, but I can make it easier for you, Slick! I'll trade you that old, broken-down white bitch for that young, pretty motherfucker Linda! I really ain't got much to lose if you knock me for that bitch!"

He was right, and he made a lot of sense. Slimy chased Linda for several more days, but he wasn't able to steal her, nor was I able to steal Denise from him.

****

Slimy started harassing Blue's girl, just like he'd done to Linda. Blue's girl Twinkles was a pretty, tall, sexy, brown-skinned girl with shoulder length jet black wavy hair. I saw Slime drive up on the curb, jump out of the car, and chase her up the street while screaming cute riddles and rhymes to make her smile and give her something to think about. It seemed like every time I saw Twinkles Slimy was right behind her screaming. At times Twinkles wouldn't walk away, so I knew she was interested in what Slime was saying. Slimy was causing problems for Blue.

Blue confronted Slimy about his advances toward Twinkles right there in front of Twinkles and all of the other players on the track. Slimy immediately started showboating. "You ain't no pimp, you're an imposter! You just popped up on the scene. You're a jail bird probably in there fuckin' fags!"

238

I saw the look of embarrassment on Blue's face as Slimy continued making him look bad in front of all of us. I knew Blue was ready to fight. Blue's body was in the position that a boxer would take only without his hands up, his left leg and foot pointed and back leg positioned for balance. Just as I thought, Blue took a swing at Slimy, but Slime slipped the punch. He must have seen it coming too. Slimy reacted with lightning speed, countering with a hard right cross, knocking Blue off his feet. Blue got up, furious, and the fight was on. Blue threw a few more wild punches but missed every one. They were quickly countered by Slimy. Eventually Mo stepped in between the two of them and broke up the one-sided fight. Slimy continued to showboat, "Yeah, pussy, I just whipped your ass like a bitch. Now Twinkles can see what kind of a bitch you really are! C'mon, Twinkles! Get out of that faggot's car and get with a real pimp. He can't even protect you."

Blue got back in his Caddy with blood all over his face. He drove off down 21st Street while Slimy was still yelling and showboating. "Your bitch ass couldn't even hit me once! You fight like a girl!"

Several weeks went by and no one saw or heard from Blue. Slimy put him out of the game. Blue was too embarrassed to show his face on the track again, especially after talking all that jail gangster shit.

Chapter 25

I sat in Crystal's apartment, lonely. I looked around at the things she left behind. The black leather open-toed shoes she bought from Wild Pair were still under the bed where she left them.

I felt terrible; my best friend was gone. My eating and sleeping habits had changed dramatically since Crystal was away. It had been over three months since I'd seen her. I missed Crystal so much. My heart was broken. I thought of things I could do to take my mind off of her. I thought about her every day.

I remembered when she said, "When it's over let's just part in peace." Maybe that was her idea of parting in peace, only I wasn't in peace.

****

I searched the internet for employment on Crystal's T40 Think Pad laptop. I sent resumes and called telecommunication and computer repair companies. I called family members to see if they knew of any companies that were hiring.

"Hey, Pete, how they treatin' ya?"

"Man, I'm hangin' in there," Pete replied.

"Any telecom companies hiring that you know of?" I asked my brother.

"Naw, man, those jobs are dryin' up. I'm about to move to Delaware; there 'posed to be an opportunity for a Network Operations Technician out there."

"When you plan on going down there?"

"I got an interview Monday morning. If I get the job I'm leaving. It's too hard to make a decent living here."

"Man, I hear ya. Pete, how's Ma?"

"She a'ight. I saw her over the weekend at Nana's. She cooked some short ribs and rice. I tore them shits up," Pete laughed.

"Aw man, don't tell me that, now my mouth is watering. Mac n' cheese too?" I remembered the way Mom would put together some scraps to make us a meal. That meal would taste better than a meal from a 5 star restaurant.

"Yeah, mac n' cheese too."

"Nooo!" I yelled, and we both laughed.

I leaned back in Crystal's black plush leather computer chair, rested my head on the back of the chair, and put both feet up on the small cherry wood computer desk. Tension left my body as I forgot about my daily stress. I cracked a smile and nodded my head in agreement a few times as Pete filled me in on what had been going on in my family. I missed my family so much. While talking to Pete I daydreamed a little, remembering the good times I used to have when we got together.

"Man, Nana wanna see everyone at the Memorial this Sunday; come around," Pete said.

The Memorial was a special ceremony given by the Jehovah's Witnesses in the first week of April every year. On that day the Witnesses met to partake in the passing of bread and wine. The bread symbolizes the body of Jesus, and the wine symbolizes the blood. It says in the Bible, "Keep doing this in remembrance of me." That is what Jesus and the Jehovah's Witnesses want everyone to do. Whoever is chosen to consume the wine and bread shall be 1 of 144,000 resurrected. There will only be 1 in every 144,000 resurrected. Whoever is chosen will know that they are chosen.

Nana had everyone meet at her house every year for the Memorial. For the past 2 years I hadn't shown up. It was a big day for Nana; she was very much into the Kingdom Hall. She was a faithful follower of Jehovah. Most of my family just went to support Nana.

Even though I went to support Nana, I tried to learn something while I was there.

"I'll try an' make it, but don't tell her I'm coming, just in case something comes up. I don't wanna disappoint her."

Pete and I spoke for at least a half an hour more before I got back to my job search.

****

I came across an interesting listing on CareerBuilder. It was for a computer repair school. Perfect; I loved fixing things. The school was a nonprofit school aimed at helping financially-challenged people in low income neighborhoods. The school was in the Bronx on Lafayette Avenue. Just my luck it was right in the middle of the Hunts Point track. I gave them a call and was told to come down for an interview the following day. I was told the school was free but space was limited, so only a select few would be allowed to attend the school. I was also told that I

would have two interviews to determine my eligibility.

The following day I went to Per Scholas dressed

very professionally. The man who interviewed me was

a short Spanish man with salt and pepper hair and gold-

rimmed glasses. After introducing himself to me he told

me a short story about his life and some of the things

he'd been through. When he finished telling me his

story I was proud of him and very much inspired. He

told me that he did a long stretch in prison and now he

was working what seemed to me to be a decent job. I

was envious. I wanted what he had. He was living proof

that it could be done, that I didn't have to break the law

my entire life in order to survive. He gave me a

glimmer of hope that someone would eventually give

me a chance, just like they did for him. When he was

done telling me about himself it was my turn to tell him

about myself. He explained to me that it wasn't an

ordinary interview and that I should try to give him as much information as possible and not to hold back. That would help him determine if I was eligible for the second interview. He wanted to hear the good, the bad, and the ugly.

Nervously, I began. "I promote prostitution for a living. I want to do other things for a living, but my options are very narrow. I want to be a professional at something; I at least want a positive title. I don't have any marketable skills, and I have two felonies on my record. I've been trying to get a job for a long time but either my record or my lack of experience is causing employers not to hire me. With computer skills at least I'll have a fighting chance. I have always been fascinated with electronics, especially computers, so I think this school would be right for me."

Talking about myself made me cringe. It was so embarrassing. But there was no look of surprise on his face. He just got up and walked to the back. I don't know who he spoke to or about what but when he came back he said, "Don't worry about the second interview. You're in."

****

I went to Per Scholas as if my future depended on it, and it did. Even on the days when I got in the house at 6am I turned around and went to school, determined not to let the streets be my only option.

I was so grateful to be accepted into Per Scholas. It was one of the best decisions I have ever made. At Per Scholas I learned all about the hardware and the software of computers. I learned how to conduct myself on an interview. I learned the proper way to write a resume. Per Scholas had strict policies and guidelines that added much-needed structure to my life. Being late was frowned upon. Being late three times was grounds for termination. Two absences were also grounds for termination.

There were four classrooms at Per Scholas, and each classroom was filled. There were approximately 30 students in each class. The students were predominately Hispanic and black. Each student had their own desk or workspace at a work bench. I sat at a bench in the front of the classroom so I wouldn't be distracted. The chairs were very uncomfortable. They were the same too-small blue chairs I had sat on in the past in public school. The ceilings were extremely high, and the walls were painted light blue. Each desk had a computer on it for each student, and we would practice on them during class. My instructor, Mr. Robinson, stood about 5'9''. He was bald, roughly 200 pounds, and African American.

"Nice coat," one of the women from the Per Scholas staff yelled one day as I hurried by her, attempting to make it to my classroom before the instructor took roll call.

"Thank you" I yelled back. I looked in her direction and forced a smile. A mink coat wasn't anything special among my peers. Most of the clothes that I wore to class were very flashy. They were my pimping clothes: way too flashy and expensive for square life.

"Everyone come to the front of the class and get your textbook," the instructor yelled just after roll call. "The textbooks are yours to keep, and so are the computers." I thought, *What's the catch? They're giving me a computer, a textbook, and a vocational skill!*

I didn't speak much to the staff or my classmates. I know they thought I was mean, but I just didn't know how to interact with squares. I didn't feel confident in their world. I was a fish out of water.

I attended Per Scholas for 4 months. At the end of the course I took a state test for my A+ Certificate. I failed the test, but Per Scholas encouraged me not to give up. Per Scholas allowed me to come back for a refresher course before I went back to the testing site to retake the test. I passed the second time.

After getting my A+ I studied at home for the next certificate. It was a little more advanced then computer repair. I studied for my Network+ and passed that one on the first try. I felt that with two certificates employers would be impressed, making my chances for employment greater. Finally I was a professional at something; I was officially a Computer Repair Technician and a Network Administrator.

Chapter 26

I took a shower and woke Linda up by yelling, "Time to make the donuts!" as I flicked the lights on and off. She got up and headed for the shower. On my way out the door I yelled, "Be ready in an hour!"

We got out about 1am. I considered it a late start for Friday night. I gave Linda $10 and told her to eat and be on the track in 20 minutes. I drove back to the track, got out, and joined Mo and the other pimps, who were already standing around there talking pimp shit. It was about 80 degrees, the sky was clear, and I felt an occasional cool breeze coming from the river a few blocks away. Pimps were pimping and hoes were hoeing. Everyone seemed to be happy and having fun. Everyone was trying outshine one another as usual.

House Man complimented me on my outfit. I replied, "Thanks, Pimpin'. I just coped it at Albee Square Mall."

There were a few more comments about my outfit. Then I heard an explosion.

Something hit me in my chest extremely hard. I looked down. My chest was red with warm blood. I knew I had been shot. But why? When I looked back up everyone was running and screaming. I looked back down at the blood dripping down my shirt in globs. I looked around and saw Slimy lying on the ground with half of his head blown away. I was in shock. I just stood there. In all of the commotion I heard someone shout, "There they go! Gray car! Follow them!" Mo and House jumped in their cars and chased the killers. Linda came running towards me screaming frantically.

"Daddy, you OK? Daddy, you OK?"

I replied, "Yeah Lin, calm down." Slimy's blood and brains looked like scrambled eggs and ketchup sliding down the front of my shirt.

Linda looked down at Slimy's body and began screaming even louder. I thought I'd better get the hell out of there or the police would be questioning me for sure. I quickly grabbed Linda by the arm and guided her to the car as I tried desperately to wipe the blood, brains, and hair off of me. Once in the car I was able to get her frantic screams down to a sob. I turned the corner on 21st and Queens Boulevard and saw cop cars all over the place. As I passed the cop cars I saw Mo's car turned sideways as if he had been in an accident. I also saw three men standing in front of Twin Donuts with their hands cuffed behind their backs. I recognized one of them as Blue.

The next day the headlines read, "PAROLED PIMP KILLS AGAIN." Blue was the trigger man.

For the next few days I knew that Queens track would be hot so I worked 11th Avenue in Manhattan. Every player was talking about what happened to Slimy. They all asked me questions because it was common street knowledge that I frequented that track. I kept my information to a minimum though. I told them that I didn't see it and that I came around after the fact.

Mo called me 2 days later with details about the funeral arrangements. Slime's funeral was held 4 days after his death. The funeral was packed. The streets were lined with Cadillacs, Mercedes Benzes, and the occasional Rolls Royce. Fur coats, *Godfather* hats, and diamonds worn by people of the underworld filled the streets and sidewalks. The place looked like a pimp convention. The Hurst that carried Slimy was white. His family's car, which followed the Hurst, was also white. His brother Dollar Bill later told me that they choose the color white because they knew Sammy would have wanted to go out showboating. I said a

prayer for Slimy that night.

Chapter 27

After putting Linda down on 11th Avenue and 24th street in Manhattan I parked my car and walked up to Jake's Deli on 25th and 10th Avenue. There were a few pimps standing around joking and hollering at hoes when they walked by. My main reason for joining the crowd was because Dollar Bill was there. Dollar Bill was a tall, light-skinned player with long, wavy hair that extended to his shoulders. His clothes were always neatly pressed and well put together. Dollar had one Chinese ho to whom he was rumored to be married. I approached the three and shook everyone's hand. I didn't know the buster that my brother had a problem with was in the group before I walked up. I'm sure he didn't know that Cash was my brother. Not many players knew that we were brothers. Dollar knew but he didn't say a word.

Just my luck, when I walked up they were talking about the incident.

"I heard some shots down there on 24th Street a few nights ago. Was that you shootin'?" I asked.

"Yeah, this fool tried to make me kill him 'bout my bitch."

"Oh yeah? What happened?"

"I drove up and this motherfucker was tryin' to rob my bitch."

"Really? Who was it?"

"Dude in the white Caddy. His hoes play 26th and 27th Streets."

Charles didn't have a clue who he was talking to. I took it as a lesson to always be mindful of whom I'm speaking to. He went on telling us the story. "I pulled my ratchet and bust off 3 shots at the fool."

"It's a good thing you checked his bitch ass. Maybe he won't come back around here."

I noticed Dollar trying to keep a straight face.

Charles replied, "He ain't comin' back 'round here. He knows what I got for him."

I tried to get as much information out of him as possible because I knew Cash would need it. I started drilling him for information. "Where you from, Pimpin'?"

"East New York."

"Yeah, me too. I'm over in Cypress Hills Projects."

"I live near Brookdale Hospital," said Charles.

I began stroking his ego. "Man, you seem to have some pretty good pimpin' behind you."

"Oh yeah. Thanks, Pimp," Charles smiled.

I had him right where I wanted him—his guard was down. After picking his brain for information for about a half hour I was ready to leave.

"I'm 'bout to check some paper," I said to no one in particular as I walked off.

I walked up to the McDonalds on 33rd Street, grabbed a burger, and called Cash.

He answered, "What up, Pimpin'?"

"Just some more a dis pimpin'. Got some news you can use 'bout that trigger-happy fool you ran into the other night."

"What ya got?"

"He gave me everything but his Social Security number. We'll talk about that in person tomorrow; where you at?"

"I'm on 1&9 in Jersey City."

"They lettin' 'em work?"

"Yeah, Pimpin', and it's on full. Massive out here, with 14 junkies, and some of them don't look half bad either. Yeah, he just came through in a white Jaguar with a full body kit, he lookin' real pimpish. I'm peelin' his ass tonight though."

"That's what you 'pose to do. I'm sure he can stand it."

Massive was an old time pimp from Jersey City. He'd only accept junkie hoes. His game was tight in New Jersey.

"Ooooh, my new bitch just walked through the door finer then a candle-lit dinner and wine. Gotta go; swing by tomorrow!"

****

I got a call from Linda about 2 minutes later. "Daddy, I'm over here at the Chelsea Hotel talking to this ho. She tryin' to come home." Linda was bringing hoes home; she finally got over her possessiveness.

"Who is she?" I asked.

"They call her Heaven."

"Put her on the phone."

A sweet, high-pitched voice came back.

"Hello."

"What's up, Baby Girl? What can I do for you?"

"Tryin' to get in where I fit in. I see you always got Linda dressed proper and you buying her a car."

I rudely interrupted, "Before we go any further, you got your chosen money, right?"

"I got $200."

"$200? Who's your folks?"

"Tommy Black."

"I know Tommy; he a Gorilla Pimp. I can't serve him with $200. You gotta come better than that, Princess. You and I both know I may have to bring my iron when I serve him his papers. Tommy got a hot head." I would have asked for more regardless of who I had to serve, even though I knew better than to serve that fool in person or without my pistol close by.

"I know; that's why I wanna get away from him. He crazy. He shot me in the mouth a few years back."

When she said that I knew exactly who she was. That news was all over the track.

"I'm interested in you, and you're making a wise choice. Hang on to my number and stack some paper. If I don't hear from you within the next 48 hours I'll assume you changed your mind."

"I'm not gonna change my mind. I've been watchin' you for a while and I really like your swag. All the hoes on the track been talkin' about you. I'm not the only one that wanna fuck with your pimpin'."

Her sales pitch was a real ego booster, but I didn't let her know it. I quickly changed the subject. "Put ya money where your mouth is. See you in 48."

"OK, here's Linda."

"Daddy, you want her?" Linda asked.

"Yeah, and when she comes home you're going on a shopping spree as a reward."

I knew Linda was going to make sure she came home, and I was going to make good on my promise.

Chapter 28

I walked up to the door and rang the bell.

"WHO IS IT?!" a deep, dry voice yelled. It was my grandfather.

"RICK!" I yelled back

My grandfather opened the door.

"Will you look at what the cat dragged in?" my grandfather yelled to everyone in the living room.

It always made me happy to see my family. They are my original team, the people who had my back unconditionally, the people that didn't want anything but to see me. It was always hard for me to be family-oriented because of the life I led. I didn't want any of my dirt to touch them, so I didn't come around often.

Clarence and his mom were at Nana's. Pete brought his wife and kids. All of my aunts were there with their offspring. There was a house full of people, and it was really nice seeing everyone again.

"Come here, boy; let me look at you," my nana said from the recliner. It was always positioned perfectly at the living room window to give Nana a good view of the street. "Boy, I'ma spank you if you don't come visit me more often."

I smiled and gave her a kiss on the forehead.

"Hey boy, what's goin' on?" my cousin Clarence mumbled from the kitchen behind me.

"Hey, Clarence," I said while smiling. I walked over to Clarence, gave him a hug, and shook his hand. I smelled alcohol on Clarence's breath. I whispered, "Hey, man, what you drinking? That smells like some expensive shit. You movin' up in the world, huh?" Both of us laughed.

"That's Hennessey. Got it from yo mama."

"My mom here?"

"Yeah, she in the back," Clarence mumbled.

Clarence, I'll holla at you in a minute."

I walked to the back bedroom to see my mother.

"Hey, Ma," I said and gave her a kiss on her cheek.

"What you up to, Rick? You ain't find me a daughter in law yet?"

"Naw, not yet, Ma. I'm workin' on it."

"Where that Crystal girl you was tellin' me 'bout over the phone?" Mom asked.

"I'm workin on her, Ma." I didn't want to go into detail. "Y'all know y'all shouldn't be drinkin' just before we go to the Kingdom Hall. I'm tellin' Nana." I dashed out of the room and headed for the living room.

"You better not!" I heard Mom yell.

"NANA!" I yelled as I quickly walked over to her.

"Yes, baby?" Nana replied.

"I missed you." I gave Nana a kiss on the forehead. I heard Mom laugh. I was always very playful with my family.

At 8pm we all jumped in Granddad and Clarence's car to go to the Kingdom Hall for the Memorial.

Chapter 29

The phone rang from a blocked number.

"You know who this is?" came from the receiver when I answered.

"Naw, who this?" I replied.

"Heaven, Tommy Black's bottom. Well, used to be. That is, if you still want me."

"Yeah, yeah, I still want you."

"Oh, I was getting scared. I know it ain't been over 48 hours."

I quickly asked, "How your paper lookin'?"

"I just robbed Tommy's stupid ass for $7,300," Heaven answered.

"Catch a cab over to 816 Ocean Avenue. Ring the top bell when you get here."

"OK, Daddy. Can I speak to Linda?" Heaven asked.

"You can speak to her when you get here."

I took a shower, got dressed, and put on my favorite cologne. I was thinking about the new car I was going to buy. I already had $33,000 stacked, and her 7 more would make 40. I'd been checking out a 1 year old Cadillac on Queens Boulevard. The sticker price was $38,000. I had to have it. I figured I could get the Cadillac for 33 cash and still have a few stacks to pimp with.

I went to the kitchen for a cup of coffee to help me get myself in gear. I had a feeling it was going to be a long day.

About an hour later the doorbell rang, waking Linda. I answered it, "Welcome home."
Heaven just smiled and walked in as if she owned the place. I immediately noticed her long, sexy legs in her tight-fitting, faded blue jeans. She wore a pair of white Nike sneakers and a white halter top. She used her hair

to hide the scar from her bullet wound. The scar wasn't bad at all. Her hair fell to about 3 inches past her shoulders and it was naturally straight. She had a Spanish look. She was very sexy. I used to check Heaven out on the track but this was the first time I got a close up look at her.

Linda just looked at her soon to be new wife in law without saying a word. I was glad she was awake to watch me break Heaven. Break was a term we used for accepting money.

I greeted Heaven, "What da deal, Baby Girl?"

Heaven reached in her bag, pulled out a stack of $100 bills, and handed them to me. I threw the stack on the couch, looked at Linda, and said, "Count it."

There was a pile of $100 bills all over the couch. Linda picked them up and started counting.

I looked at Heaven and said, "Relax, you're in good hands. You made the right choice."

About 10 minutes later Linda shouted, "$7290."

I gave Heaven a long, hard look. "Where's the other $10?"

She looked confused. "You told me to take a cab."

Heaven was right, but I didn't apologize.

I picked up the cash, put it in my inside jacket pocket, put my jacket on, and took Heaven to her new home.

****

When we approached the building I held the door for Heaven; a little chivalry never hurt. We approached the apartment; I unlocked the door and once again held it open for Heaven. I handed Heaven a set of keys and welcomed her home. It felt weird giving Crystal's apartment to Heaven. It seemed so final.

Heaven inspected the place, then came back to the living room and said, "Thank you. I promise you won't regret it." She gave me a big hug. It was a long hug, way too long, as if the apartment was a real big deal to her.

I had to ask, "Where did Tommy have you living?"

"I lived in the tiny, unfinished basement with 3 other girls. We didn't have any heat or hot water. There were just a few mattresses on the floor. The place was filthy."

"So why you just leavin'?" I asked.

"I've been wanting to leave him for a long time, ever since he shot me, but I didn't have any place to go. I didn't want to choose another pimp and end up in an even worse situation. That's why I studied you for so long."

"You're OK now, Heaven. You're free to come and go as you please. Stay true to the game, respect your home, and you'll be OK."

Heaven gave me another hug. "Thank you, Slick."

"You're welcome. Now, what's Tommy's phone number? It's time to break the news."

She gave me the number, and I saved it in my phone. I figured I would have to do it alone.

I walked to the store on Flatbush Avenue while dialing Tommy's number. The phone rang once before he answered, as if he was waiting by the phone.

"What da deal, Pimpin'?" He automatically knew who it was.

I gave him the news. "Yeah man, Heaven showed up at my house 'bout an hour ago crying 'bout some trick who robbed her. She said she can't go back home cause you'd kill her."

"Where's the bitch, man?"

"She in my basement in Harlem right now." I lied to him in case he wanted to look for her. I continued, "I don't really want her; she only chose with $200, and I know that's not enough to serve a real pimp. So if you want her back I'll bring her back to you." I knew he wouldn't take a handout, even if he needed it. Pimps were very prideful.

"How much the bitch had?" he asked as if he didn't hear me the first time.

"200 punk-ass dollars," I answered.

There was a long silence. Then he said, "Naw, I don't want the ho. I just thought the bitch stole something from me."

"Well, what is it, Pimpin'? I'll strip-search her and bring it to you if I find it. You know you my man, and I ain't gonna let no broad come between us," I said, smiling because I knew I'd conned him.

Tommy was too embarrassed to tell me that he got robbed for over $7000. He probably didn't even know who robbed him, since his whole stable left at the same time while he was asleep.

I went back to Heaven's apartment and prepped her for the night.

"You gonna let him get me?" Heaven asked. Her eyes widened, and I could see the fear in them.

"Naw, you straight. I just got off the phone with Tommy. He accepted his papers like a real pimp."

I saw the look on her face change as she calmed down. I drilled instructions into Heaven's head for about 15 more minutes before leaving her to enjoy her new home.

Chapter 30

I went back home and took $26,710 from the safe to make an even 34 grand. I put the money in a knapsack. It was the 90s, and I knew that I just couldn't walk into any car dealership with $34,000 and buy a car without expecting to end up in handcuffs. However, this particular car dealership took a liking to pimps. They were a Jewish -owned car lot on Queens Blvd not far from the Mets Motel. They knew we made a lot of money and we'd spend it with no problem. They always broke the money up to make it look like we were making payments.

I ran downstairs, excited because I was about to make a big move. The money I was carrying made me feel invincible and powerful. When I got to the dealership I had the knapsack filled with money in my hand. I was ready. I think the shady car salesman knew I was ready too.

"Ready for that Caddy?" he asked when he saw me.

I answered "Maybe" as I looked around at other cars, trying to stay cool. I walked in the office, and Jack was sitting there at his desk as usual. Jack was another shady car salesman. He was an older man, approximately 50, with gray hair and a goatee. He held an unlit cigar in his mouth as he spoke to me.

"Hey man, where you been? You don't come around no more," Jack said as if he missed me. I knew it was just part of his con. He continued, "Mercedes, Range Rover, I got a nice Rolls Royce in the back for 150 grand."

I walked up to him, emptied the bag on his desk, and said, "I want the white Caddy in front. There's thirty four thousand there."

Jack replied, "No way. That caddy is $38,000. I bought it for 33. I'm only making a grand, no way."

I picked up my money, put it back in my bag, and placed my business card on his desk.

"The same car is about a mile up the Blvd. I'm gonna see if he'll take the thirty four. It's blue—I really had my heart set on white, but I'll settle for blue if I have to. If you happen to change your mind before I get there give me a call and we'll make the deal."

I took my bag and walked out of the office, got in my car, and took off. Before I even got to the corner my phone rang.

"It's Jack. Come on back," Jack said with his raspy voice.

"You got it, Jack," I said as I smiled and hung up the phone.

I parked my car behind Jack's car lot, grabbed my knapsack, and within 2 hours I was driving off the lot in my new ride.

The Caddy was real nice. Pretty white Sedan Deville, burgundy interior, fully loaded, white soft leather top, and factory chrome rims. I really enjoyed the ride home.

****

When I got home Linda was asleep. I took my shower and got dressed in my brand new double-breasted, white suit made by Calvin Klein. I had a burgundy and white handkerchief in the breast pocket, a pair of two-toned burgundy and white alligator shoes, and a burgundy and white necktie. The only thing that was missing was the hat, but I knew I was still the man.

After I got dressed I woke Linda up.

"What time is it?" she asked.

"Time to make the donuts," I answered as I stood in the mirror popping my collar.

"Daddy, you look nice," Linda said in her soft, sexy voice.

"Don't I?" I replied, full of myself.

Linda was dressed and ready in about an hour. We walked downstairs, and when I got to the car Linda asked while smiling, "When did you pick this up?" I ignored her and we got in.

We picked up Heaven and drove back to Queens. The girls and I were enjoying all the amenities the car had to offer. By the time the girls realized we weren't going to Manhattan we were already in Long Island City.

"Daddy, I'm scared of the Queens track. I still have nightmares about that man that got his head blown off," Linda said when she saw where we were.

"We working in Queens tonight." We really weren't, but I wanted to fuck with her. Must have been the devil in me.

"But Daddy I don't wanna work out here," she whined.

"Get out of the car!" I yelled as I pulled behind my other car. Linda didn't even notice my other car. She got out with tears running down her cheeks. I gave Linda the keys to my old car and said, "It's yours."

She stood there in shock for a minute with her hand over her mouth. Then she started smiling, with tears still running down her face. She hugged me and kissed me all over my cheeks. My cheeks were red with lipstick.

"Y'all go to Manhattan," I told her, kissing her on the cheek.

Linda was a happy ho. She finally got that car I promised her. Legally the car still belonged to me, but I don't think she cared.

****

I went to 8th Avenue to show off my new ride. I drove up 8th Avenue very slow with the music blasting to make sure everyone saw me. I pulled over on 43rd and 8th Ave to talk to Preach.

"What they do, Preach?" I yelled from the window.

"Slick, you did it again, huh? That's a pretty Caddy! When you knock it?"

"Picked it up this morning on Queens Blvd."

"What it run you?"

"34, man. Hop in; let's bend some corners."

Preach got in the car, looked around, and caressed the seats as if they were a woman. He played with the radio and all the other buttons and gadgets on the car as we took a ride downtown.

"Man, it's lookin' a little hot out here," I said.

Preach agreed. "They lookin' for Tommy Black. I heard one of his girls robbed him and he killed her. The police found her in the basement of his house chained to a radiator, with a steering wheel club lock shoved up her ass. The steering wheel lock cut her liver, causing her to hemorrhage and bleed to death."

"No!"

"Yeah, Tommy's on the run. I don't know why they lookin' for him out here, though. He'd be a fool to be out here."

I thought about Heaven and the shit I would've had to deal with had I told Tommy the truth.

"Wow, that's that bullish, Preach," I responded. I didn't like to curse around Preach.

"Yeah, you know Tommy a fool. If they catch him he gonna hold court in the street."

I drove around in silence for a little while thinking of all the sickos the game produced, including me. Somehow I felt it was partially my fault that the girl lost her life. I shook my head sadly while holding my forefinger and thumb on the bridge of my nose. I imagined the girl begging for her life and trying to convince Tommy's crazy ass that she didn't steal his money. When I came to a red light at the intersection of 29th Street and 11th Avenue, I prayed silently. *God grant me the serenity to accept the things I cannot change, the courage to change the things I can, and the wisdom to know the difference.* I took a deep breath and sighed. I was full of more bad feelings that I would have to suppress.

Preach asked, "Where your brother, man? I haven't seen him in a while."

"He layin' low out in Jersey."

"1 and 9, huh?"

"Yeah, ain't nobody there but Massive and his junkies."

I drove around Manhattan with Preach for about another hour before dropping him off on the corner of 8th Avenue and 45th Street.

****

I parked my car and walked up to the Burger King on 48th Street and 8th Avenue. When I entered there was a pretty little black girl with chubby cheeks waiting to take my order. I flirted with her for a while before ordering.

"What a man gotta do to have a pretty woman like you?"

She smiled from ear to ear.

I spoke with her for a while, and she seemed to take a liking to me. I thought, *Cool, I can move this broad*. According to her name tag her name was Lisa. Lisa had a shoulder-length black weave, pretty brown eyes, a cute little fat ass, and a chocolate complexion. She handed me my food and didn't ring it up. I thought, *She likes to give, that's a plus*. I figured I'd work on her for a few weeks.

I visited Lisa at her job every day for a week. By the end of a month she decided to quit her job and take on a new career: a life of crime.

Lisa was already a whore. She did everything a whore did. She even dressed like a whore, but she didn't get paid for it. Within 3 days I had her making over $400 a night. She was a good moneymaker, but I didn't feel I was controlling her emotions enough. She had a lot of loose ends that needed to be tightened. I knew if I took her on a road trip it would help us bond. I thought Miami would be a long enough road trip for me to get to know her.

Chapter 31

"Wake up! Pack your bags!" I yelled one Saturday morning after having my coffee. Lisa and Linda woke up.

"Daddy, where we goin'?" Linda asked.

"You go back to sleep. I'm 'bout to put some mileage on your new wife in law."

"Where y'all goin', Daddy?"

"Miami."

"Just you and her?"

"Yeah, you off the hook this time."

I knew that was good news for Linda because she hated Miami. Every time I took her she complained about the air being too humid.

"Check my bread while I'm gone." I always left Linda in charge while I was out of town.

Lisa didn't have a problem with the sudden unplanned trip. She took a shower, got dressed, and packed her bags. Lisa was excited because she'd never been out of New York City. I knew she felt she was going more on vacation than to work.

****

Before leaving town Lisa and I stopped by Heaven's place. Heaven was upset. She heard about Tommy Black murdering her ex wife in law. She wouldn't speak much, and her eyes were bloodshot red. I knew she'd been crying all night. I walked over to her and gave her a caring huge. I knew the timing was wrong because of the spectator but I also knew I had to do it.

"You OK, Boo Boo?" I whispered as I held her tight in my arms.

"Daddy, that was meant for me. I caused it to happen," she cried.

I shook my head. "No. He's a sick bastard, and I know for a fact she wasn't the first person he killed."

"But it was over the money."

"How do we know that? They haven't caught him," I replied.

I held Heaven for a few more minutes to make sure she was OK before I left.

****

I drove half the time and Lisa drove the other half. There were so many beautiful states we passed through on our way to Miami but I liked Georgia best. We stopped in Atlanta for a layover. It was similar to New York City but there wasn't all of the hustle, near-misses from taxi cabs, and rude people who find it hard to even say hello. The streets were clean, the air was fresh, and the atmosphere was very serene.

Lisa insisted on going out to get a few dollars as soon as we got there. She took a shower and got dressed in her tight black spandex dress with her black 6 inch open-toed platform stiletto heels. She put her makeup on, and her nails were, as always, in perfect condition, with a French tip manicure style. As she sprayed her expensive Armani perfume on she looked at me in the mirror.

"Daddy, can I have some cock when I get back?"

I replied, "Ask me with money in your hand." She sucked her teeth and poked her lips out.

Lisa finished getting dressed and walked to the track. She worked while I slept.

I got a call from Lisa early the next morning. "Daddy, you gotta come get me! I just robbed the trick. I'm under a car on Bradford St. I don't know where to go!"

I didn't know how to get there so I quickly got dressed and went to the front desk to ask for directions.

When I finally found Bradford Street I gave Lisa a call. "Where you at?"

"You just drove past me; I'm under the black Expedition in the middle of the block. Make a U turn."

I made the U turn and drove slowly down Bradford Street. I heard her scream before I saw the SUV.

"Daddy, over here!"

I made another U turn and double-parked near the Expedition. Lisa came out from under the car. She was wearing a pair of jeans that were at least two sizes too big for her. She had dried blood on her face, and she was dirty from lying on the ground. She was a mess.

She got in the car panting. She was out of breath and excited.

"Daddy, I got him!" she yelled while reaching in her inside pocket for the huge bank roll that she just robbed the trick for. I didn't have time to count it; I wanted to get away from the area because I knew the trick was probably looking for her.

"How much is it?" Lisa asked as she threw the large stack on my lap.

"Just be cool, I'll count it in a second. What the fuck happened to you?" I replied.

"I hit him with the knockout drops, Daddy. When he fell asleep I went for his pants 'cause he was on top of my skirt. Then the motherfucker woke up. I guess I didn't give him enough. He grabbed me by my hair. I kicked him in the nuts and screamed 'rape' at the top of my lungs. Security came, and I ran out the door as soon as they opened it." The excitement on Lisa's face told me that she really got off on robbing people. "No cabs would stop for me looking like this so I hid under a truck. He would've had to kill me to get that money back."

"Now that's what I like. A bad-ass Brooklyn broad!"

"Daddy, I'ma getcha paper."

"Yeah, you did good." I kissed her on the cheek. Lisa loved validation. That's just one of the things I learned about her during our trip.

"Now can I get some cock?"

I thought my heart would stop; I had forgotten all about that. Although I was happy about the money I wasn't looking forward to going to bed with her.

"Yeah I'ma fuck your brains out," I replied, as I cringed and my stomach turned from the thought of having sex with her. It wasn't that she wasn't pretty, it was just that the things I witnessed in the game turned my mind from sex. Besides, I was very picky about who I slept with, and Lisa didn't turn me on. She was a little on the heavy side and just a tad too short. I was tired and didn't feel like tricking my body to have sex with her by thinking about Janet or the money she

made. I was far from broke, so prostituting myself to

her was not going to happen, at least not on that night.

As I got closer to the hotel I thought of ways to

get out of having sex with Lisa. We stopped by a soul

food restaurant before getting to the hotel. They had

everything—ox tails, pig feet, collard greens, macaroni

and cheese—and the people that owned the place were

very friendly. When we got back to the hotel Lisa took

a shower, I rolled a blunt, and we ate. After dinner Lisa

fell asleep, and I was a happy camper.

I counted my stack while she slept. I always

liked to count my money alone. Counting money was

one of my favorite pastimes. I'd count my money

several times; I just loved the feeling. Lisa told me that

I swayed my body from side to side unconsciously

while I counted money. While I was counting I realized

she was right. $3600 was her take. It turned out to be a good night.

I took off my clothes quietly so as not to wake Lisa, then got in the bed beside her while cursing myself for not getting double beds. Thank God I didn't wake her.

****

When I woke up Lisa was on top of me giving me oral sex. I viciously pushed her to the floor while yelling, "Get the fuck off of me!" I heard Lisa hit the floor hard. I knew I hurt her but I didn't care. I was furious.

"Daddy, I raped you," came from Lisa as she laughed hysterically.

Her laughter made me angrier. My eyes were blood red. I got up and looked around for my underwear while she continued laughing. Once I found my underwear I headed for the bathroom to brush my teeth. When I came out of the bathroom Lisa was still laughing and teasing me.

"Daddy, that was good," she said as she laughed some more.

"Fuck you," I replied with passion. I couldn't believe she violated me like that. I couldn't believe she was that horny. If I looked at pussies all night at work the last thing I would want to look at would be another one when I got home. I told Lisa, "If you ever do something like that again I'ma break my toe off in your ass!"

****

Heaven called me. "Daddy, that buster that your brother had beef with keep sweatin' me."

I replied, "What you tellin' me for? Get away."

"Daddy, you know I don't call you for no bullshit. That clown won't let me work. He all up in my face."

There was a short silence as I thought about how to handle Charlie.

"I'll call you back in about 30 minutes."

"OK, Daddy."

I took a quick shower, threw on my light blue Enyce sweat suit with my white high top Air Nikes, straight out of the box. I didn't even tie the sneakers because I was deep in thought, and I didn't want to lose the idea. I rushed out of the room and called Heaven back.

"I want you to get wit' him."

"What?!" Heaven yelled.

"You heard me right. Get with him."

"Daddy, what I do? You don't want me no more?"

"Naw, you gotta take one for the team."

She immediately knew what I was talking about. "Oh, we gonna have some fun with his bitch ass! I'm down, Daddy. What you want me to do?"

"Break him off $300 for a choosin' fee and stay with him until I get back. Change my name in your phone to 'Danny the Trick' in case he wants to inspect the phone. Just give him enough money to keep him eatin' and stash the rest. You should still have a stack for me when I get back. Keep track of the amount of money you give him because I want you to take it back from him the next day. If you make $400 you stash $200, give him $200, and have him spoil you with $150. Just leave him gas money. Put it in his left hand and take it out of his right."

"OK, Daddy, I can do it," Heaven replied.

"Call me every day about 2am, you should be down by then."

"OK, Daddy."

"See you in a few days." I hung up without saying goodbye.

****

While chatting with an old New York player on the track, Lisa walked passed me on the opposite side of the street in a brown halter top, a beige mini skirt, and some 6 inch thigh-high leather boots. She kept her hair well-groomed and neat. I never had to tell Lisa that it was time to go to work. She looked forward to it.

I hung out on the corner until about 3am, when the track seemed to slow down. I called it a night; besides, it seemed like a good hour to get on the road. I knew I could make it to Miami by the following evening. On my way back to the hotel I saw flashing red and blue lights on a small dark one-way street. As I passed the street I looked down it. It looked like Lisa was going to jail. I thought, *Now what am I going to do? I don't even know where the courthouse is at.* I looked again; it looked like Lisa was fighting with the cop. I walked away before the cop saw me and put 2 and 2 together. It would have been a long night for me too. I continued walking to the hotel thinking, *Why don't she just go to jail peacefully? She probably won't get more than a fine, and I'll come get her in the morning.*

****

I got a call from Lisa. "Daddy, the last date I caught was a cop! After the date he pulled a badge out and told me I was under arrest. He took the money back out of my bra, so I picked the used condom up off the street and told him, 'If you arrest me your ass is in trouble too, 'cause I'm taking this condom filled with your DNA to court with me.' Daddy, he called for backup and his buddies came. A crowd was developing so I knew had witnesses."

"You crazy!" I shouted.

Lisa continued, "The cop walked over to talk to his buddies and came back to me and said 'OK, you can go.' I told him 'No, I'm not going nowhere 'til you give me my $60 back. I'm gonna file charges against you unless you give me my money.' He walked back over to his friends to discuss it and then started feeling around in his pockets for my money. He gave me the $60 back and let me go."

"You crazy out yo head, girl," I laughed.

She had to be crazy to pull that shit.

When Lisa got back to the hotel we laughed about the incident for about a half hour, then we packed our bags and continued to Miami.

****

The phone rang and I answered. It was Charlie.

"What up, Pimpin', dis Charlie Rock. I den got you for that bitch. Bitch said she wanna be with a real pimp. She just push me three hundred and she down for my crown."

I knew Charlie was around a lot of people by the way he was showboating over the phone. I asked him, "Who you got me for?"

"The one that's not comin' home," he replied.

"Well, let me talk to her to make sure it ain't no kidnappin'." I was playing my position.

Charlie continued showboating. "You should've spoke to her when you had her! Now I got her, and I'm speakin' for her. Stay up, Pimpin'." He hung up on me.

I laughed out loud when I hung up. It really tickled me to know what kind of sucker Charlie was.

I immediately gave Cash a call.

"What da deal, Cash?"

"I'm out here on 1&9 knockin' Massive left and right for those junkie hoes."

"I'm playin' yo boy Charlie Rock outta pocket. I just set my game up in his camp."

"Ooohh, don't tell me dat! We got him?"

"Yeah we got him. We talk when I get back. Just thought I'd put a smile on your face."

"I'm smiling, Pimpin'. Hurry up and get back. Please hurry."

****

When we got to Miami we checked into the President Hotel on Collins Ave. Lisa was so excited she didn't even sleep. She never slept when we got to a different city; she had to explore. She changed clothes and headed for the beach, which was only two blocks away.

I smoked a blunt and ate the rest of a half-eaten sandwich I'd bought on the road. Then I lay down and watched a little television before dozing off.

****

BOOM BOOM BOOM.

Someone was banging on the door frantically. It scared the shit out of me. I got up and sprang into action. I grabbed the weed and half-smoked blunt off the dresser and headed for the toilet. The last thing I needed was another drug charge.

BOOM BOOM BOOM. They banged again as I was flushing the shit.

"Who is it?" I yelled, already knowing it was the police.

"Lisa ! Let me in!" Lisa answered.

Goddamit. I'd just flushed all of my weed.

"Why you knockin' like you crazy?" I asked. I was now very upset. I know she heard it in my tone of voice.

But Lisa was excited. "Daddy, I just robbed the dope boy on the first floor. He been tryin' to get in my

305

pants all day, so I gave him some, put his ass to sleep, and got him."

She threw a stack of bills and a plastic bag filled with about 3 ounces of high-grade cocaine on the bed. I grabbed the money, neatly put it together, and counted it.

"Daddy you rockin'," she giggled.

"$1900! You a pretty good thief, huh?"

I thought, *This girl is a fucking klepto.*

I knew I couldn't stay in that hotel anymore because the dope boy lived downstairs. After drilling Lisa for details about the dope boy I felt it was a good idea to stay in for the rest of the night.

I asked, "Did he see which way you ran? Does he know you're in this hotel?"

He knew she was staying in the hotel but didn't know which room.

Lisa and I stayed in for the rest of the night and played chess.

****

My phone rang. It was Heaven. "Daddy, please come home. I'm tired of payin' this buster."

"How is everything goin' otherwise?" I asked.

"I'm fine, Daddy, but I wanna go home."

"Calm down, Heaven. I'm packing as we speak. I should be there within the next 48hours. What you got for me?"

"$800."

"Cool. Hold that and stack some more. See you shortly," I said just before hanging up.

After I packed our bags and stashed the money and the coke we got back on the road, New York bound. I knew with a girl like Lisa I had to keep moving. She was the first real thief I ever had.

It took us two days to get back. I didn't want to speed since I knew I had enough money and coke in the car to get us both twenty years in prison. We alternated driving, the same as we had on our way to Miami.

Chapter 32

Linda greeted me at the door with a hug. "Daddy, I missed you."

"I missed you too, babe. Where my bread?" I really did miss her, but I had gotten so money-hungry that my money was the first thing on my mind.

"Just a minute." Linda went in the bedroom and came back with a plastic bag. "There's close to $3000 there." She handed me the bag.

I could tell Lisa was exhausted; she dropped her bags and lay down on the couch without taking her clothes off.

The trip paid off. Linda had $2900, Lisa made $6300 altogether between flat backing and robbing tricks, and I knew that Heaven had anywhere between $800 and $1200.

****

Heaven called at 2am sharp. "Daddy, you back yet?"

"Yeah, I'm back. This is what I need you to do. Steal his keys between now and tomorrow. Make an extra key and leave it somewhere for me."

"Daddy, he made me a key; you can have mine," she replied.

"Even better. Where can you leave it for me?"

There was a short silence, then she answered, "There's a mat right outside of his door. I'll leave it under the mat."

"What's the address?"

"252 Dumont Ave."

"Cool, see you tomorrow."

"OK," she laughed just before hanging up.

The following night I called Cash, and he met me at the address. Everything was going smoothly. The place was well-kept with expensive furniture. Cashmere checked every room with his 9mm in his hand. After making sure the place was empty we relaxed and made ourselves at home. Cashmere made himself a sandwich. We both kept our latex gloves on because we didn't want our fingerprints in the house. We waited all night.

Heaven texted me at 6.30am. "B there in 5 minutes we're parking."

I told Cash to get in position. Cash stood on the left side of the door and I stood on the right. We both stared at the doorknob intensely, waiting for it to turn. I cocked the trigger back on the old 32 revolver that Cash had given me for the occasion. Anxiety raced through my body; my heart pounded in my chest. Tiny sweet beads formed around the wrinkles between Cash's eyebrows, and his eyes revealed the soul of a cold-blooded killer.

Approximately three minutes later I heard Heaven's loud mouth coming down the hall. Charlie put the key in the door and opened it halfway, as if he knew something was wrong. Then he came rushing through the door after Heaven shoved him hard. He tripped and fell on his way in.

"Get your faggot ass in there!" Heaven shouted.

Cashmere was right on point with the barrel of his 9mm on Charlie's temple. When Cashmere cocked the trigger back I knew it was over for Charlie Rock.

To my surprise Cash ordered him to get up.

When Charlie got up he looked at me and began to realize what happened. "Oh shit, you set me."

CRACK. Before Charlie could finish the sentence Cash smacked him in the nose with the gun, knocking him against the wall.

Cash grabbed Charlie by the shirt and guided him to the kitchen. Cash reached in the cabinet and took out a box of white rice, then escorted Charlie to the bedroom.

Heaven ran towards me screaming, "I missed you, Daddy!" She hugged and kissed me all over. We spoke for about 5 minutes before I asked, "What you got for me?"

"Including what I stashed tonight I got $1100. Charlie got money in the safe, Daddy. I don't know how much or the combination."

I pushed her off of me and walked to the back. On my way to the back I heard whimpering. "Please don't kill me, I'm sorry." When I walked in I saw Charlie in his underwear sweating and crying while he kneeled on rice grains.

I could tell he was in pain from every little rice grain cutting into his flesh. Cashmere was getting pleasure out of the torture he was putting Charlie through. Every time Charlie couldn't take the pain any more he would put his hand on the floor to take some pressure off of his knees, and Cash would burn him with a cigarette butt until he removed his hand. I couldn't believe what I was seeing. Cashmere was a sick motherfucker. I interrupted.

"You know he got a stash in the closet."

"Yeah? How much?"

"Don't know, and the broad don't know the combination."

"What's the combo, Charlie?" Cash asked Charlie as I walked towards the closet and found the safe.

"OK, just don't kill me. 28, 30, 28," Charlie stuttered.

I tried the numbers but they didn't work.

Cash burned Charlie's cheek with a cigarette butt, then put the barrel of the gun on his already broken nose. At that point a foul odor came over us, as if something was rotting. Something in that closet just wasn't right. I thought maybe there was a body in the closet. I looked at the two of them, and Charlie had shit himself. There was brown milky shit running down the inside of his thigh, and the white rice he knelt on had turned brown.

Cash acted like he didn't smell it. "I'ma give you one more chance to keep your life, Charlie. What's the combo?"

"28, 48, 28," Charlie answered between sobs.

The numbers was right. He had a nice stack of cash and about a half a kilo of coke. I ran to the kitchen, got a plastic bag, came back, and emptied the safe. Then I went back to the living room with Heaven.

I got a text from Cash. "You guys leave now; I'm gonna finish up. Call me tonight."

I escorted Heaven to the door and told her we were leaving. As soon as we got in the car, we heard two shots ring out. Heaven just looked at me. Neither of us said a word. I started the car and took Heaven home. It was a silent ride all the way home.

When I got Heaven home I went to the bathroom to count my money in private. There was $22,300 stacked neatly in rubber bands.

Chapter 33

"Man, I just got a better job!" Pete sounded so excited. "The job opportunities are much better out here. You might want to come out here and search for a job. From what I hear they are only running background checks for the state of Delaware. I know you been arrested in every state, but are you clean in Delaware?" Pete laughed.

"I think so." I didn't see the humor in his question.

"The price of living is a lot cheaper too. I just rented a 3 story house for $1100 a month. That's unheard of in New York. Why don't you come down for a weekend and see what Delaware has to offer?"

I agreed to come down the following weekend.

A few days later I went to Delaware to visit Pete and look for an apartment. It wasn't long before I saw one that I had to have. It had wall-to-wall carpet, central

air, off-street parking, two bathrooms, two bedrooms,

new stainless steel appliances, and much more.

"How much is the rent?" I asked the rental

agent.

"$750 per month," she replied.

I looked at Pete.

"Told you," he said while smiling.

An apartment like that would have cost me at

least $3000 per month in Brooklyn. She had my

attention.

"What's the procedure for renting an

apartment?" I asked the agent.

She replied, "It's 1 month rent, 1 month

security, and a $200 deposit on your heat."

She showed me several apartments before we

went back to the rental office. At the office the agent

explained a little more about the place and the procedure to move in.

"Can I take an application with me and mail it back along with my ID and deposit?"

"Sure," the agent said with a big smile on her face, probably because she knew she made a deal. She more than likely got a commission.

The following day I filled out the application and sent several money orders to the rental office totaling $1700.

****

For some reason I didn't want to be around women. I needed a place where I could be alone. Since Heaven was in Crystal's place I didn't have a place for getaway time. I checked into the Liberty Motel on 11th Ave and took a nap.

I woke up around midnight and called Linda. "What's up, Lin?"

"We down, Daddy."

"That's what I liked to hear."

I lay back down for another hour before going out to the track. I stepped out into the night to smell the cool, tainted air that came from the meat factories on the West Side. I drove up 10th Ave and ran into a junkie whore. She was coming out of the store on 10th and 28th St.I knew she was a junkie by the track mark on her neck. Her hands were swollen and her jeans had blood spots on them, but she was very pretty. Pimps used to always brag about their white girls making double the money black girls made. I couldn't help it; I had to seize the opportunity. Tina was an opportunity knocking at my door. I opened it mainly for security reasons. I thought, *If Linda and Heaven decide to leave, Tina will be my backup plan.*

Although I didn't want to pimp anymore, I had to. It was my only means of support. I thought about quitting over and over again, but I didn't have the courage to walk away from the game without having some other means of financial support. Eventually I knew I would have to make that move. I knew I had to make it fast or something very bad was bound to happen.

I pulled over and she walked toward my car. I asked her from the window if she knew where I could cop some dope. She got in and directed me to the dope spot. She said her name was Tina. She never asked me if I was pimpin'; she probably didn't care as long as I got her some dope.

"You gonna take care of me, right? I'm sick," she said as she lay back in the seat as if she was out of breath.

"Sure, Baby Girl. You got your needle?"

"Yeah, you got yours? Turn right here."

She assumed I got high on dope too.

"I snort," I replied, just to assure her that I was a user because I wanted her to feel comfortable.

"Right here. It's in the building. You want me to go get it?" Tina asked.

Without answering I got out of the car and followed her up to the building to cop my own dope. I never trusted dope fiends. I coped 3 bags and told the dealer that I'd be back before the night was over for a bundle if it was good. I made sure I said it loud and clear so Tina could hear me. I knew the dope was the only reason she was with me, but that was OK because money was the only reason I was with her.

I took Tina back to the hotel with me. I gave her two bags and stashed the other one. I went to the bathroom and made a sniffling noise as if I was snorting the third bag. When I came out she was preparing her dope. She went into the bathroom to shoot it. When I heard her say, "Damn, that's some good dope," I knew she was finished.

Tina walked out of the bathroom with the exposed needle in her hand.

"Baby Girl! You gotta put that needle away."

"I'm sorry," Tina apologized, then put the cap on the needle and put it away.

"It's OK, just be a little more careful," I replied, while staying far away from the needle.

"Can I lie down for a few minutes?" Tina asked with her voice dragging as if she was already feeling the effects of the heroin.

"Lie down, get comfortable," I replied.

I finally got a white girl on my team, and I could see for myself how much money they made.

Tina lay down and quickly fell asleep.

****

"Tina, wake up! Time for your medicine!" I yelled as I pulled out the other bag of dope that I had stashed away. I knew she'd be sick when she woke up.

"Thank you... You so sweet," Tina said as she got up to shoot her wake-up bag.

It was time to put Tina to work, but I needed to pick her brain for a little information and give her a new program first.

"We gotta talk while you getting off, Baby Girl. I need to know what da deal is with you. Who ya folks?"

"Massive," she answered.

"Massive? Why he got you out here among sober hoes? He usually keeps you dope fiend hoes out in Jersey City on 1&9. Why are you here in the Big Apple?"

"Please, my vein is running away. I promise to answer any questions as soon as I'm done," Tina replied.

When Tina was done in the bathroom I got up and took a long, hot shower. When I came out of the bathroom Tina was sitting on the edge of the bed nodding with an exposed needle in her hand and a bloody tissue next to her. There was no way I was getting back in that bed.

I became upset because I just spoke to her about her carelessness. Then I realized it wasn't her fault; that's just the way she lived. I took a moment to reevaluate my relationship with her. I asked myself over and over, *Do you really want to take on this responsibility?* I came to the conclusion that the money she made that night would be my final deciding factor.

"Wake up!" I yelled, loud enough to startle Tina.

Tina stood up as if I scared her. "I'm up," she replied like a robot and started gathering her things, including the needle top.

"Don't you got something to explain to me?" I asked Tina.

"What?"

"Why are you out here in the city?"

"I met a trick in Jersey City that had a lot of dope; he took me to his house and we were getting high for 3 days. His money ran out so I went out to make some money before calling Massive."

"Why didn't you just make some money and go back to Jersey City? Massive got your medicine."

"Honestly, I got stuck out here. There's so much drugs out here I couldn't leave. Every time I got Massive's money the dope would call me."

I knew Tina was being honest. I already knew what she confirmed.

"I got plenty of dope," I said, "enough to feed an army of fiends. So if you want to get down with me let me know. We can start tonight."

"Sure, I'll get down with you: as long as you promise I'll never be sick."

I figured she'd be down as long as I had her medicine. Dope fiends never care about anything but staying well. They will put dope before everything. Sober hoes wanted to go shopping, buy new cars, and have their own apartments.

I headed out the door before she finished her dope because I knew that one bag wasn't enough for a dope fiend just waking up, and I wasn't in the mood to hear her beg for more. I went to the front desk to pay for another day at the hotel. Then I went to the dope spot that Tina hipped me to. I picked up a bundle and was back to the hotel within a half hour.

When I got back Tina was nodding again. It seemed like I was always waking Tina up.

"Wake up!" I yelled, startling her. "Here are two more bags. Don't do them now. Go get some money; I wanna see what you're made of. I'll be back in a few hours. Have my bread right."

Tina gathered her belongings, didn't jump in the shower, and didn't ask for a toothbrush or a change of clothes.

"Daddy, can I have your phone number?" she aksed. "I should be back in about two hours with your bread. Where should I stash it?"

"In the phone book," I replied and gave her my number. I didn't bother serving Massive. I figured it was the norm for a junkie to run off, and he wouldn't be worried about her. He'd probably expect it.

Tina brushed her hair and walked out the door.

****

The ride to Brooklyn was relaxing. I stopped at Junior's Restaurant on Flatbush Avenue for a slice of cheesecake on my way to Heaven's house.

"Hi, Daddy. There's $490 in the foot of my pantyhose," Heaven said as soon as I woke her up.

Heaven got up to go to the bathroom in the nude. She was gorgeous. Her body was just the right size and height. Her legs were long and smooth, and her tits stood straight up in the air. I started getting excited. It'd been a long time since I met a woman who turned me on despite the things I witnessed in the game. I figured, *What the hell; I got a little time and a condom in my pocket.*

While Heaven was in the bathroom I peeked in her purse on the dresser. There was the usual woman stuff in it: makeup, tampons, tissue, phone numbers. Then I noticed a pill bottle. I thought, *Here we go, another junkie.* The label read AZT. I knew that medicine was given to AIDS patients. When she came out of the bathroom I told her what I'd done.

"Heaven, I peeked in your bag. How long you been sick?"

There was a long silence before she spoke. "I had it since the early 90s." She went on to explain. "When I lived in Cali I joined a gang. In order to get in I had to be fucked in. Every man in the gang fucked me; that's how bad I wanted a family. I'm not 100 percent sure, but I think that's how I got it. One of the guys that fucked me in was a famous rapper. He died from AIDS."

I gave Heaven a kiss on the forehead.

"I'm scared," she said just before she broke down crying.

Damned, I hung my head low. I wished there was something I could do to make her pain go away. Passion and empathy filled my heart. I looked up at the ceiling and silently asked God, *What did this poor girl do to deserve a death sentence?*

I gave Heaven a caring hug until she finished crying. Although her naked, sexy body was up against mine I wasn't in the mood anymore. I stayed in the house with Heaven until I felt she was emotionally stable.

****

After picking up my money from Lisa and Linda I headed back to Manhattan. I hung out with Preach for a few hours before going to the hotel. When I got there the room door was open. I walked in to discover Tina nodding out on the toilet bowl. There was a bundle of dope and three crumbled-up dollar bills on the floor next to her, and she clutched an exposed needle in her hand. Her pocketbook was emptied out on the floor. There was no way I could have Tina representing me.

"Tina!" I yelled.

She woke up instantly, but she was having trouble speaking, and her eyes only stayed open for about 30 seconds before she dozed off again.

"Tina, how much money you got?!" I yelled.

Tina replied, "It was slow out there. I blanked."

That meant she didn't catch one date. But it was obvious she had made enough money to buy dope. I was upset watching her as she sat there on the toilet nodding with dry blood on the tissue in one hand and an exposed needle in the other. Her head nearly touched her knees, and there were track marks all over her arms.

Looking at her, I felt myself become angry at my father. Tina sitting on that stool brought very bad memories to mind. I remembered my father sitting on the stool with a needle in his arm when I was 12 years old. How could he have been so selfish and put a needle in his arm knowing he had two young boys to raise? I stood there for several minutes just thinking about all the cowardly things my father had done, all the misery he had brought my family. I longed to see him because I owed him an ass-kicking. I hated him. I don't think I've ever hated anyone as much as I hated him. The anger was overwhelming.

I unzipped my pants, pulled my dick out, and pissed on Tina's head. She looked up at me. "Why you doin' that to me?" she managed to ask as the piss trickled down her face. Then she nodded off again. I zipped my paints up and left her there to enjoy her high.

Chapter 34

I headed to midtown to see to see if Preach was still out. As I was driving up 10th Ave I thought a black Chevy was following me, so I made a right on 38th Street. They made a right too. I made a left on 8th Ave; so did they. They were definitely following me. As I crossed 42nd Street I saw two cruisers coming my way with their flashing lights on. I stopped in the middle of 8th Avenue between 42nd and 43rd Streets.

The cops in the unmarked car behind me got out first. They ran toward me with their guns drawn, and the cops in the cruiser did the same. One of the cops screamed,

"Get the fuck outta the car with your hands up!"

When I got out of the car there was four guns pointed at me.

"Get the fuck on the ground, face down, face down on the ground!" was the next order I heard.

I got down on my knees, and one of them pushed me all the way down until my face was touching the ground. Someone grabbed my hands and forced them behind my back. I felt the cold, hard handcuffs tighten around my wrists. The cops lifted me to my feet.

"You're under arrest for murder," they said.

The ride to the precinct took forever, with the policemen asking questions trying to pry information from me. I knew better than to talk to them. My mind was racing. *Did Heaven snitch? It couldn't have been Cashmere; he pulled the trigger. How much do they know?* I was going through some serious motions.

They put me in an 8x10 foot cell. It was filthy, and there was graffiti all over the walls. There was someone's leftover breakfast under the dirty metal bench that I was supposed to use as a bed. It smelled like piss. There was vomit in the sink. But I had to make the best of a nasty situation, so I lay down on the hard metal bench and stared at the ceiling for what seemed like hours until I feel asleep.

I was awakened by the loud noise of the correction officer yelling, "Food up, fellas!" I got up and sat closer to the bars because I knew from past experience that I would be receiving my meal through the bars. The ugly white police officer stood in front of my cell and said, "Get used to it: you gonna be here for a while. By the way, your brother got the worst end of a shootout in Jersey City with the police last night. He's dead."

His words hit me like a ton of bricks. I sat motionlessly on the cold, hard bench for hours, absorbed in my own thoughts. I thought, *I am leaving this life. I'm going to Delaware as soon as I'm free. I'm throwing my cell phone away and I'm starting a new life.* The pain I felt was like nothing I ever felt before. I wanted to cry but I couldn't. My nerves took over my body, and my legs started trembling out of control. I was a nervous wreck. For the next three meal calls I didn't even touch my food. I had no desire to eat.

An officer came to my cell to take me to the next building, where I was placed in another cell to await my first court appearance. The cell was much bigger, but it was packed with people, all African American and Spanish. People lay on the floor and bench; they sat on the sink; some just stood. Some of the people were obviously homeless. I took my position in the rear left corner. I sat on the floor, not caring about the trash or the junkie who lay down beside me. My mind was far away from that cell. I was grieving the loss of my brother.

I recognized the bum lying next to me as Tommy Black. Tommy was filthy. His shirt and pants were badly soiled, and his hair looked as if he hadn't combed it in a month. He had a full beard, and he desperately needed a shower. If it wasn't for the huge mole on his nose I probably wouldn't have recognized him.

I woke him up. "Tommy, Tommy Black."

Tommy woke up and stared at me. "Slick?"

"Yeah, man. How long you been here?"

Tommy replied, "Man, I been sitting here for nearly a week. They're giving me extensive bull pen therapy. You heard 'bout what I did to that prosecutor's daughter, right?"

"Prosecutor's daughter?" I repeated.

"Yeah, Slick, the bitch's parents are heavy hitters around here. Her mom's a DA in the Queens Supreme Court and her dad's a State Trooper."

"No shit?"

"Yeah."

Tommy sat up as if he was in pain. At the same time he held his stomach, and I noticed a huge white bandage wrapped around his torso.

"What happened?" I asked while pointing to the bandage.

"I shot it out with Five O. When I ran out of bullets they ordered me to come out with my hands up. Slick, I knew I was facing life. I wanted to take my own life but I didn't have any more bullets. I pointed the gun at one of the pigs and he shot me in the stomach. They took me to Bellevue. Just my luck I survived. I laid up in intensive care for two weeks before they brought me here. Pig came to my bed in the hospital last week before I got here and gave me a razor. He told me to cut my wrists 'cause it would be my only way to freedom, and to be honest with you, Slick, I thought about it. Not only did they charge me with murder, but they charged me with sodomy. You know a sex crime is the worst charge you can have up north."

I replied, "Damn, Tommy. Look like they got a pretty good grip on me too."

"I'm hip. I heard about that shit that went down with Charlie Rock. I didn't know Cashmere was your brother. Police was talkin' about that shootout this morning. I'm happy and I'm remorseful 'bout what happened to him. I'm happy 'cause Cash ain't facing an asshole full of time like I am. I'm remorseful that he's no longer with us. Cash was a good pimp."

Tommy looked at the floor. His eyes got watery. I knew the pain he was feeling because I was feeling the same pain. I could tell Tommy was weakening mentally. His situation was becoming too much for him to bear.

Tommy continued, "I wish that was me. I wish I could trade places with Cash. Cash got the easy way out. Why couldn't that pig be a better shot? I gave him a clear shot; now I gotta ware a colostomy bag for the rest of my life, and God knows what other kinds of shit I gotta put up with up north."

I knew it didn't look good for Tommy, but I tried to give him some words of encouragement. "Don't worry, Tommy. They still gotta prove you did it, so it ain't over. You might walk outta here. Have faith: the Pimp God ain't gonna let two good pimps go down like this. We gonna come outta this smelling like a rose, watch what I'm tellin' you. By next month I'ma run into you on the blade and smoke one witcha, you watch." I didn't believe one word I said, but it sounded good and I'm sure it made him feel better.

I still don't think Tommy knew who stole that money, and even if he did he was in no condition to do anything about it. Heaven and that money were probably the last things on his mind.

The guard yelled "Movement!" and everybody stood up. He started calling names for court. Tommy's name was on the list. I shook Tommy's hand before he left and gave him a few more words of encouragement.

Finally there was room in the cell. About an hour later an investigator came to see me. He told me that I was being charged with murder. He said that the DA was sure she has a solid case against me. He wouldn't give me many details. If Cash was dead then the only other witness they could've had had to be Heaven. My bail was set at $500,000 cash or bond. I could've at least come up with 10 percent, but cosigners were a problem. Living the life I led for so many years I didn't know too many people with legitimate jobs.

I called Linda at home. Everyone was still in place and still making money. They were just waiting for me to get home. I was driven to Rikers Island. I knew I had to stay there until I could make bail or until my next court date, whichever came first.

I called Linda every day for a week. She said that pimps were after all of them like vultures. They were hollering, "Your man ain't never coming home; we don't allow renegades out here. Choose up."

The pressure was on.

Lisa eventually went back to her mom. The most important people I needed were Heaven and Linda. As long as Heaven was on my team the prosecutor couldn't use her against me, so what could the prosecutor possibly have?

Linda got me a good attorney with the money I had stacked. She told me that the lawyer informed her that if she tried to bail me out without a job she would end up in jail trying to explain how she got the money.

I went to court for 6 months. Every time I went to court Linda and Heaven were there. Finally during

343

the 7th month the judge set a trial date. The next time I went to court would be for trial. Linda sent me my gray two piece double-breasted suit and my black alligator shoes.

Chapter 35

February 16th 2010, Manhattan Supreme Court. I went before the Honorable Judge Leonardo. My lawyer assured me that Heaven was still with me so they didn't have a witness as long as everything happened exactly the way I told him. I walked out into the dimly-lit courtroom to see the jurors whom I had selected the week before. My mom and brother were also in the courtroom. I'd asked Linda and Heaven not to come to the trial. I thought their presence might make me look bad. Some people can spot a ho a mile away.

My lawyer was awesome. He was a high-profile Jewish lawyer. Linda got me a Jewish attorney because it was rumored that they got the most respect in the courtroom. He was in his mid 50s. He stood about 6'2" with a bald head and a full gray beard. He was considered to be one of the best lawyers in New York City. The prosecutor was young, in her early thirties. She was Asian, and she stood about 5'5". She wore a two piece brown suit and low beige pumps.

The prosecutor went on for hours trying to make me look like a bad guy, and my lawyer did his part in trying to make me look like an innocent righteous citizen. After approximately 4 hours my attorney made his closing statement, wrapping it up. There was a recess, and the jury was to come back with a decision within an hour. I sat on pins and needles for that hour.

When the jury came back in with their decision the guard yelled, "All rise!" We all stood, honoring the judge.

"Be seated!" the judge shouted.

My heart was pounding. Every hair on my body stood at attention, and I was sweating bullets. I knew that the next few seconds would make a huge difference in my life. I closed my eyes, folded my hands underneath my chin, and prayed.

Another guard read, "Based upon the evidence presented, we find the defendant innocent of first degree murder."

I heard my mom and brother rejoicing.

After seven long months of built-up anxiety I was finally able to relax. My breathing slowed down. My muscles began to cooperate. The tension in my back and neck disappeared. My heart rate slowed down to a normal rhythm. A sudden peacefulness and calmness overcame me. I was finally free after seven long months! I folded my hands under my chin once again and thanked God for answering my prayer. Then I remembered my plan. I was done with the game. It was time to start my new life.

I turned around to walk through the small wooden gate that separated me from my family and gave my mom and brother a hug.

"Meet me in the hallway!" my lawyer yelled as the jury left through a door next to the judge's chambers.

As soon as I walked out into the hallway two tall white men in black suits walked up on me.

"Ricky Smalls?" one of them asked.

"Yes," I replied.

"You're being rearrested for the murder of Crystal Foy. Crystal Foy's body was found on Jones Beach in Long Island. Authorities sorted through her cell phone records, and we are sure she was involved in some illegal activity, under your instructions, that contributed to her death."

At that point my whole world came crashing down. The only woman that I ever had feelings for was gone. She was dead, and it was partly my fault. It wasn't fair to me, and it definitely wasn't fair to Crystal.

"Mr. Smalls, turn around and put your hands behind your back," one of the officers demanded.

I did as I was told. There was a hollow, dark hole growing in my soul as I hung my head low, stared at the floor, and slowly walked back into the court room. I heard my mom screaming and saw Pete looking on in disbelief.

The officer who guided me back into the courtroom stopped me in front of the judge and read me my Miranda Rights. The other officer explained to my attorney what was going on after my rights were read. Then the officer who spoke to my lawyer repeated to the judge what he told me in the hallway. I couldn't believe what I was going through. I'd just awoken from a nightmare, and another one was already beginning.

Everything was happening so fast. I needed an explanation; there had to be a logical one. I briefly analyzed my situation. The obvious answer came to me as if a light bulb had been turned on in my head. The Scripture that Preach used to always remind me of came to mind: *You shall reap what you sow.*

I didn't look back as I was led away. I could hear my mom screaming.

Once I got to Rikers Island I was strip searched. I was ordered to hold my testicles up, squat, and cough. Then I was placed in a large cell with several other men who had either blown trial, violated parole, or had new cases. There were four cells in intake: three for normal inmates and one for suicidal inmates. Each of the normal cells had approximately 10 people inside, crammed into benches or lying on the floor. The suicide cell had 1 person inside; he had self-inflicted wounds all over his arms. I stayed in intake for 2 days without taking a shower or changing my clothes. All of us reeked of body odor. When I finally got to population I took a hot shower in an open shower area. It was one large room with approximately 20 showerheads coming out of the wall and a drain in the middle of the floor. After my shower I went to my 8 by 10 foot cell to grieve. My cell consisted of a bench, a toilet, a stool, and a desk. Everything in the cell was metal and either affixed to the wall or to the floor. Graffiti was all over the badly-chipped gray walls.

I'd lost my appetite again. I stayed in my cell for nearly a week, rapidly losing weight. I just lay there thinking about the direction my life had taken, about Cashmere and Crystal. When I finally got over the shock I wrote letters, read books, and exercised to help me cope with my situation.

For one year I fought the murder case until Crystal's murderer was caught. He was a serial killer who was known for calling women who advertised on Craigslist, establishing a relationship with them, and then murdering them.

Chapter 36

When I was released I had nothing: no job, no hoes, and no income. Everything I'd gotten out of the game I gave back to the game. The only one I had to rely on was my mother. She'd moved into the apartment that I was renting in Delaware before I got arrested. We lived of off Mom's $900 per month Social Security check for 5 months. It wasn't very comfortable for two adults: we were hungry, and our bills were piling up. Still, we got by.

"Wow, you sound so nice over the phone. I'll bet you're very pretty." I flirted with the customer service representative of the heating company. I heard her giggle, so I knew I put her in a good mood. I held my forefinger to my lips as a sign for Mom to keep quiet. She was laughing; she always got a kick out of the way I handled the bill collectors. "What did you say your name was?" I asked.

"My name is Katie. And yours?"

"My name is Rick, Ricky Smalls, and I'm single." Katie giggled again. "Well Katie, the reason I'm calling is because I got a shut-off notice from you guys today, and due to the down economy I'm really struggling. Today I have a huge decision to make. I could either buy food and Pampers for my newborn child, or I could give you my last little bit of money and hope you will keep the heat on. I'm a single parent and the only person my son has. It's just him and me against the world. I am hoping and humbly asking you to keep the heat on just long enough for me to make some sort of payment and payment plan. I can make a payment on the 25th of this month. I just got a new job and my first paycheck is due on the 25th. Is there anything you can do?"

Mom had to run out of the room; she couldn't hold the laughter any longer.

"Awww. How old is your son?" Katie replied.

"He's 3 months. Kept me up all night."

"Yeah, they will do that, Mr. Smalls. Just a minute; let me take a look at your account and see what I can do for you."

"Sure, take your time." I knew I had her. I was very confident when it came to negotiating deals.

Katie came back to the phone in less than 2 minutes. "When did you say you could make a payment?"

I walked out of the room toward the kitchen where Mom was washing dishes and gave her a smile and thumbs up. She smiled back, shook her head, and continued doing the dishes.

"I'll send you at least $100 on the 25th, and I'll send you $50 a week thereafter until I'm all caught up."

"OK Mr. Smalls, that will be sufficient. Just let me notate your account so you won't have any problems."

There was a short pause. I sat on the bed and thought about what I was going to tell the next bill collector.

Katie came back once again. "OK Mr. Smalls, you are all set. You take care, and take care of that baby."

"For sure Katie, and thank you for being so understanding. Enjoy your day."

Next I called the electric company: "Good evening, Kevin, how's your day so far? My name is Ricky Smalls, and I just received a shut-off notice from your office. I recently lost my job over at the Ford dealership, and I really want to pay you guys but I'm just going to need a little more time. I have applied for unemployment but was denied because I was just two weeks short of the required employment time. Welfare has accepted my application though. My first check isn't due to come 'til the 25th. Is there anything we can do to work this out so I can get a little more time?"

"Unfortunately, Mr. Smalls, there isn't much we can do. You are already three months behind on your bill. You did say you were on welfare though. There may be something you could do to at least buy you some time. There is a program associated with welfare called The One Shot Deal that may be able to help you. I don't know if they will approve you, but they normally approve people in your situation. With your welfare paperwork as proof that your One Shot Deal is pending we will extend your service. You must get the paperwork to us before the shut-off date though, so hurry."

Chapter 37

Going to welfare was humiliating. Never in a million years had I thought I would resort to begging for financial support, but it was either beg or take my chances in the streets. My life had made a complete 360 degree turn. I was back to living below the poverty level.

Poor, desperate people sat around waiting for their names to be called. Toddlers and infants yelled and cried. Surprisingly, the staff was all very polite. Everyone was given a clipboard as soon as they walked in. There were white walls covered with posters, a receptionist's desk directly in front of the entrance door, and a waiting area behind the desk. To the left were a dimly-lit hallway, an elevator, and several offices. To the right were more offices.

I stood on line in front of the receptionist's desk with other people who had hit bottom. I filled out an application and to my surprise the same dreaded question was on that application: *Have you ever been convicted of a felony?* I lied, figuring I'd at least get The One Shot Deal before they caught me.

"Ricky Smalls!" the interviewer yelled, then gestured for me to follow her. "Hello Mr. Smalls, have a seat. Tell me, how can I assist you?" the interviewer asked very professionally.

"I need some assistance paying my bills and I don't have any food in my house." Hearing myself utter those words was weird. It had been a long time since I'd been penniless.

"OK Mr. Smalls, just let me take a look at your application."

I gave her the application, and there was a short silence while she read it. I felt horrible. My pride and dignity were shattered. I started getting angry: angry at myself as well as the system.

"Mr. Smalls, how were you supporting yourself up until now?"

"I've been locked up for the past 19 months," I answered.

"And before you were incarcerated?"

I came clean. "I promoted prostitution."

There was a look of shock on the women's face. I bet she wasn't expecting to hear anything like that for an answer.

I continued, "Miss, I don't wanna break the law anymore. I don't wanna go in and outta jail, but I can't find a job, and my back is against the wall. I'm not here because I wanna hustle the system. I would give anything not to be here asking you for a handout."

At that point tears began to come to my eyes. The expression on the woman's face changed to a sympathetic one. She handed me a box of Kleenex.

"Miss, may I please shut the door 'til I can get myself together?"

"Yes, shut the door."

I rambled on and cried for about 5 minutes, not giving a damn about my image. I was a broken man. My spirit was broken. I was beat all the way down.

"So this is what it's come down to: I have to beg. I am at your mercy. I can't even be a man and take care of myself. You have no idea how hard it was for me to come here. I have always supported myself. People look at me like I'm stupid 'cause I keep breaking the law and getting locked up. What the hell am I supposed to do? A forty-two year old black man with multiple felonies. Who's gonna hire me? I'm all set up to go back to prison!"

I realized I was yelling and that I may have been going too far. I dried my eyes and regained my composure. After wiping the tears from my eyes I looked up at the woman. What I saw took me by surprise: she was crying too.

"My son is in the same situation," she admitted to me. "He did the only thing he knew how to do to survive. He'd been looking for a job since his release from prison three years ago. No one would hire him, so he went back to selling drugs: the only job that was available to him. He was arrested, and he violated his parole. They sent him back to prison with a new charge. It will be at least 10 years before he's free again. Now the system is moving to evict me because my son got arrested with drugs in the hallway. If anyone in public housing is arrested for a drug offense their policy is to evict the entire family." She continued, "I know the system isn't fair, Mr. Smalls, but just hang in there. Something positive will happen."

When we were done venting to each other the woman opened the door. She was a professional again. She took copies of my identification then she told me that she'd be right back. She had to go to the basement to get me some food.

She gave me her cell phone number and told me, "You're only supposed to get one bag of food per week, but take this bag of food and meet me in the back. I'll bring you another. If you run out of food give me a call and we'll meet out back; I'll bring you more. Don't worry about your one shot deal; I'm gonna push your paperwork. Mr. Smalls, you are doing the right thing. Consider this a resting period until you can come up with a plan. Breaking the law is not a good plan. It's only going to make matters worse."

She identified with my situation and wanted to help me. Her willingness to break the rules to help showed me that there were people who really cared and who were going through tougher times then me. She showed that my situation wasn't unique. Every one of those social workers probably had similar problems.

Chapter 38

Somehow I found the strength to continue looking for a job. I was determined to find a job. I kept putting my resume out. I asked family members for their help and support. Auntie lent me her car, and Pete gave me a suit to wear on interviews.

I asked one of my neighbors for a job. He was the manager of Domino's Pizza. He told me to come in to the shop Monday evening and I could start delivering pizza Monday night. I explained my situation to him, and he told me not to worry about my background.

Monday evening I showed up, took a short aptitude test, and was handed my uniform. I was a pizza delivery man. I was grateful for the job. My job at Domino's Pizza was a stepping stone, a step in the right direction. I continued looking for other work in the day time.

The money I made at Domino's Pizza wasn't enough. I couldn't catch up on my bills, and the gas company eventually turned the heat off. Mom and I went for months with no heat.

"YOU'RE SLEEPING IN THE LIVING ROOM TONIGHT!" Mom yelled from her bedroom.

The living room was right next to the kitchen. Mom put a huge pot of water on the stove and boiled it so steam would heat the living room just before I went to sleep. In the morning Mom boiled water again for her bird bath. I dealt with the cold showers. That went on for nearly six months.

"Mom, what are we gonna do?" I asked her one day. "We can't keep living like this."

She said, "Don't worry, change is comin'."

I'm not sure if she said that to keep me calm or to keep herself calm, because there were many days when I saw a look of worry on her face as well.

One day during my job search someone told me to come in for an interview immediately. It was a little computer repair shop on the border of Pennsylvania and Delaware. When I got there the manager asked me a few computer-related questions. I remember one of them was "What would you recommend as a good backup and restore program?" I didn't have an answer for him because I had never used a program to backup and restore files. So I said, "I'm sorry, I don't know of any."

I thought, *He's probably questioning my skills now. I blew it...* Even though I'd never used a backup and restore program, the question was so trivial that I should have had an answer without hesitation. It was a question I'd studied when studying for the A+ exam.

He handed me a laptop and told me to break it down and take the motherboard out. I did as he asked, and he was impressed.

"You did that in seven minutes! You're hired. Come downstairs and let me show you where you'll be working."

Pete was right: employers were a little more lenient in Delaware.

There were six monitors on a bench in the middle of the floor, computer parts and accessories all over the shop, and two other technicians down there working on computers. It was great; a computer technician's dream come true. I beat myself up a little on the way home for not knowing the name of one backup and restore program, but it didn't matter: I had a job!

After working in that little shop for four months I was ready to take on any computer repair job. There wasn't a computer problem that I hadn't seen. I could diagnose computers from just hearing the symptoms. I loved the work. The experience I was getting was great too, but I still had to find something else, something that would generate more cash. There were times I would bring home less than $200 for a week's work, my salary was commission based.

I planned on staying there until a higher-paying job came along, but after 6 months reality set in. If I got another job it would never be one that I could make a decent living from because of my criminal background. Even with the certifications I held it would never be enough: society just didn't want me. I was part of society's lowest caste, a group of people that society had forgotten about. No one gave us decent jobs; we'd be lucky if we got a job mopping the floor. I was stuck at that computer repair shop making below minimum wage. I looked at the bright side, though: I was doing something that I enjoyed, and I was getting hands-on experience. Despite the difficulties, I knew that I was doing the right thing. I was finally moving in the right direction. I wasn't making much money, but it felt good to be making a living without breaking the law. To hell with society—I was proud of myself.

But there was something missing in my life. I began to miss hustling. I used to enjoy the hunt of looking for prospects and leads. I craved wheeling and dealing. I had hustle in my blood. I thought, *If I could just put the two together, computer repair and business, I can't lose.*

I thought for a long time before I finally quit the computer repair job with nothing but a plan to start my own business. I had two things in my favor: I was ambitious, and I was at the bottom. That left me only one way to go: up.

I still had my laptop. I had a prepaid cell phone, a house phone, and a round glass table just big enough to sit the laptop on. I looked for nationwide computer repair companies over the Internet. I knew that if a company was serving the whole nation it was likely they needed help. I called and emailed every computer repair company I could find.

Craigslist's "Help Wanted: Technical Support" section had hot leads because those employers revealed that they were in need of my help. I sent each potential business partner a short and simple proposal explaining the benefits of hiring me as a subcontractor as opposed to hiring an employee. I gave them the impression that I had several technicians on my team. I could be anybody I wanted to be over the phone. I was the CEO of A Plus Technicians, a rapidly-expanding computer repair company that serviced the tri-state area.

From the time I'd sold my first television to Chico I'd been in business for myself, so I knew starting my own business wasn't just a passing fancy for me. I had more than enough experience. Many people in my situation have to think outside of the box to survive. I had been thinking outside of the box for years, so it wasn't anything new for me. For years, while others were resting and taking it easy, I was putting in work. I was used to putting in 12 hour work days. I'd even gone for several nights without sleep because I was doing so much business in the street, so I was definitely ripe for the task.

There were times when I felt like taking a break, but I'd take a good look at my situation and get back to work. I'd look down at my mattress on the floor, think of the cold shower I'd have to take in the morning, and pick up the phone to call more companies.

****

"Good morning, may I speak to Mr. Smalls, please?"

"Yes, this is Mr. Smalls. How may I help you?"

Damn, I thought, *why in hell did I answer the phone? I know it's a bill collector.*

"Hi, this is David Jenkins of TNR Industries. I'm sorry it took so long for me to get back to you. You sent us an email last week concerning some contract work that you may be interested in doing for us."

"Yes I remember." I really didn't. I had sent so many emails.

"Why don't you tell me a little about your company and what you do?"

I was prepared for that question. "We run Cat 5 and Cat 3 cables for analog and digital systems. We terminate, test, and troubleshoot cables, desktops, laptops, and servers. There are 5 of us serving South Jersey, Pennsylvania, and Delaware. All of my technicians are multi-certified and capable of handling large projects on short notice."

"Really? That sounds like a company we'd like to partner with. We have over 200 sites that need computer upgrades and at least 20 of them are in your area. It's a simple swap. We have all of the material on-site, so all you would have to do is a clean swap and upgrade the software. Does that sound like something you'd be interested in?"

He bought it.

"It depends on when you'd like us to begin," I replied. "We are all booked for the rest of the week." I knew it wouldn't take me but a few days to find available technicians. A lot of people were looking for work.

"We are flexible as long as you have your area finished by the end of the month."

"Sure, Mr. Jenkins; we can handle it. We can start Monday morning."

"That's great, Mr. Smalls! I'm going to send you a contract. Fill it out immediately and return it with a copy of your business license and business insurance.

Is it OK if I reply with an attachment of the contract to the original email that you sent us?"

"Yes, that'll be fine, and I'll get the paperwork back to you as soon as possible."

"Thank you, Mr. Smalls. Have a great day."

"You do the same, and thank you for the opportunity."

Finally, hard work and perseverance paid off. I was in business.

****

I called Pete.

"Hey Pete, how they treatin' ya?"

"I'm hangin' in there."

"Yeah, sometimes that's all you can do."

"How's the job hunting comin' along?" Pete asked. Sometimes I thought he was looking for a job for me just as hard as I was.

"It don't look good for the traditional 9 to 5; that's what I was callin' you 'bout, though. Someone just offered me some work as a Field Technician, but I'm going to need a business certificate and insurance. That's gonna cost me. Can you help me out? I'm strapped for cash."

"How much do you need?"

"I'm not sure yet. I'ma look into it today."

"What is this, independent contracting?"

"Yeah, how you know?"

"Because you need a license and insurance. A friend of mine on the job does the same work on the side: he installs and troubleshoots phone systems. He's always bragging 'bout how much money he makes per ticket. That's definitely the right move. You won't have to worry 'bout anyone askin' 'bout your criminal background, and you can make your own hours. Find out how much and get back to me, I gotchu."

I knew Pete would help me out if he had it, especially if he knew it was for something positive.

I got my business license, insurance, and the signed contract back to TNR within 48 hours. I put a help wanted ad up on Craigslist looking for Field Technicians to cover the tri-state area, and just as I thought people were responding to the ad before the day was over. I hired 5 Technicians within 3 days. I hired 5 because I knew at least 2 of them would back down at the last minute; that's just business. I gave a short verbal test over the phone, and if they passed I had them send a copy of their driver's license to me via email. By Monday evening I had a letter of acceptance from TNR, 30 tickets from TNR, and 3 Field Technicians ready to close the tickets.

The feeling was great. I was on to something. Knowing that what I was doing was working inspired me to work harder. By the end of two months I had contracts with 7 national computer repair companies.

Today, I hire underprivileged inner city youth, recovering drug addicts, and ex-cons. It gives me a good feeling to know that I can help make a difference in someone's life. My employees get skills, money, and a feeling of self-worth. It keeps them off the streets. Not only is it a humane thing to do, but it's also a good way to keep the crime rate down. Most people who break the law do so because they don't have a choice. They've been denied welfare, housing, and job; what else are they going to do? I know that some of them are going to screw up, but they are going to screw up because they are human, not because they are ex-cons or drug addicts. They aren't bad people; they are people who need chances. Many are hardworking employees with talent just waiting to be utilized.

I always tried to be fair with my technicians when it came to the amount of work they were getting and the time it took for them to get paid. Unfortunately I wasn't always able to be fair because I learned that some of the companies I was doing business with were struggling financially. Some companies weren't able to pay me on time, and since I relied on their checks to pay my technicians, sometimes my technicians pay was late. As time went by I figured out which companies were not in my best interest to do business with.

In my first year I made over $100,000, which in my opinion was OK for a four man team in the beginning stages of a business. For the first time in my life I felt successful. Not successful because I was making a lot of money, because $100,000 gross between 4 technicians is not a lot of money. I felt successful because I didn't have to break the law in order to survive.

I finally caught up on all of my bills. I got the heat turned back on first. I donated food to a few churches, and my own fridge stayed filled with food. Sometimes I'd splurge and buy some expensive seafood or prime cut steaks for my mother and me. I took Mom out to eat at restaurants of her choice. I was able to give Auntie back her car and buy one of my own. I bought a Hyundai Elantra. I paid $1600 for that car, and it felt better than buying a Cadillac for $38000, because every dime of that $1600 was made legally.

Today, I pay taxes. I deal with people in a totally different world then the one I am accustomed to. I work directly with Fortune 500 companies. I deal with some serious issues. People depend on my company to come through for them daily because my company and the people that work for me are very important.

I am now a positive role model. I got a text from my daughter on September 4th 2012. It read, "Happy birthday to you, Dad. You're the best dad in the whole wide world. Love you Pops." To me, that is success. I got all choked up and had to show Pete. I forwarded the message to him. My daughter is so dear to me I couldn't even include her in this story. The last thing I want is for someone to kick my past in her face.

I am in my 2nd year now, and my goal is $300, 000 for the year. I have opened up a computer repair shop in Ridley Park, Pennsylvania to supplement my income and give my technicians work when the subcontracting tickets slow down as they sometimes do.

Chapter 39

I despise people who get out of ghetto and never look back. Not only do I look back, but I go back. I will never forget people like Mrs. Thompson who fed me when I was hungry. I wish I could give her a hug and tell her how thankful I am, may she rest in peace. I eat at the very few soup kitchens that are set up in the ghettos to feed poor people because when everyone else rejected me, those were the people who accepted me. I do everything I can to let them know that they are somebody too. I never want anyone to feel what I've felt.

I have spent nearly two years writing this book because I care about ex-cons and the people that are locked into the ghettos. I want them to know that they still have a chance despite the obstacles that they have to overcome. I also want ex-cons to know that they don't have to feel any less of a man or woman because they are ex-cons. Jesus was an ex con.

A lot of times ex-cons need encouragement from people who identify with their situation. A little encouragement can go a long way; there is no way I would have made it this far without encouragement. I'm hoping this book will encourage them to look deep within themselves and find their talents. Everyone has talent. Many ex-cons find their talent in jail. While incarcerated for a short bid I met artists, singers, fitness instructors, boxers, and writers. There are so many talented people in the penal system. Wesley Snipes is even in there.

The United States Judicial System is set up for people in the poorest communities to be incarcerated at an early age, and society is set up to keep them in bondage by discriminating against them upon release, thereby leaving them no other option but to break the law and be re-incarcerated. I don't know of one person that doesn't make mistakes. How could anyone turn their back on a person who only wants the basic necessities to survive, like a decent job, an education, and shelter? It's hard to believe the United Sates is a democratic country. Something is terribly wrong with our system.

I often wonder if police, lawyers, and judges can sleep well knowing that what they are involved in is hurting people. They know dammed well what they are doing is equally as wrong as what I was doing, but they called me the scum of the earth.